GW01048661

Foreign investment in Eastern Europe

Foreign investment in Eastern Europe

Zbigniew Dobosiewicz

London and New York

First published 1992
by Routledge
11 New Fetter Lane, London EC4P 4EE

Simultaneously published in the USA and Canada
by Routledge
a division of Routledge, Chapman and Hall, Inc.
29 West 35th Street, New York, NY 10001

Laserprinted by LaserScript, Mitcham, Surrey
Printed and bound in Great Britain by
Biddles Ltd, Guildford and King's Lynn

British Library Cataloguing in Publication Data

A catalogue reference for this book is available from the British Library

ISBN 0–415–05688–8

Library of Congress Cataloging in Publication Data

Dobosiewicz, Zbigniew.
 Foreign investment in Eastern Europe / Zbigniew Dobosiewicz.
  p. cm.
 Includes bibliographical references and index.
 ISBN 0–415–05688–8
 1. Investments, Foreign – Europe, Eastern. 2. Investments, Foreign – Law and
legislation – Europe, Eastern. I. Title.
HG5430.7.A3D63   1992
332.6'73'0947 – dc20   91-5093
                                                                  CIP

Contents

Figures

Tables

0   200 km

GERMANY

P O L A N D

● Warsaw

SOVIET UNION

Prague ● C Z E C H O S L O V A K I A

CZECH

AUSTRIA

SLOVAKIA
■ Bratislava

● Budapest

H U N G A R Y

R O M A N I A

SLOVENIA
Ljubljana ■

● Bucharest

■ Zagreb
CROATIA

● Belgrade

BOSNIA
Y U G O S L A V I A

■ Sarajevo

SERBIA

B U L G A R I A

MONTENEGRO
■ Titograd

● Sofia

● Tirana
ALBANIA

■ Skoplje
MACEDONIA

ITALY

TURKEY

GREECE

———————— Frontiers of East European states

-------------- Frontiers of autonomous republics

●   Capitals of states

■   Capitals of autonomous republics

Map of Eastern Europe

Introduction

The concept of 'Eastern Europe' was introduced after the Second World War and is now used interchangeably with 'East-Central Europe' to refer to the countries (other than East Germany) that used to be called 'people's democracies', namely Poland, Czechoslovakia, Hungary, Yugoslavia, Romania, Bulgaria and Albania. These seven countries form a sizeable part of Europe and are the home of 125 million people. Their geographical location (particularly in the case of the first three) is such that developments in this area significantly affect the political situation in the world and the global balance of forces. That was the case in 1944–8 when communist takeovers in these countries resulted in the forging of a powerful communist bloc: without Eastern Europe the Soviet Union would be an isolated country with limited leverage. Again, when a tide of change swept across Eastern Europe in 1989–90, it precipitated the breakup of that communist bloc; in consequence the division of the world into Eastern and Western camps ceased to exist. What for well over forty years had been perceived as a threat by Western Europe disappeared.

A new political and economic order is coalescing in Eastern Europe and a process of evolution from a communist to a capitalist system is under way. One symbol of these changes can be found in Warsaw where the first stock exchange was opened in 1991 in the old headquarters of the communist party, and the Ministry of Ownership Changes, which is supervising the process of privatization, is housed in what used to be the censorship office. A new system is being put in place in the seven East European countries, which is increasingly similar to that in Western Europe and whose hallmark is political and economic pluralism. In these changes a significant role is being played by external factors, one of which is foreign investment.

Transformation of the economic system in East European countries is a very formidable undertaking beset with resistances and blocks. Some of them are hard to overcome. Foreign investment and the operation of foreign enterprises can be likened to a battering-ram beating down the many obstacles to the introduction of a free-market economy that for over forty years the old system has chosen to ignore. For both the old state sector, still powerful, and the new but swiftly growing class of private entrepreneurs foreign enterprises also serve as a model. Their superior efficiency, productivity, and profitability create a potent 'demonstration effect' whose influence is increasingly felt in the political sphere as well.

The rapid growth rate of foreign investment in Eastern Europe in the 1980s should not obscure the fact that until 1989 its actual scale was very small. In 1990, however, that began to change, the size of foreign investment multiplying to produce a qualitatively new situation. In 1991 foreign enterprises and joint ventures in which they have a stake have already begun to play a significant role in certain branches of the economy. It is likely that a continued influx of external capital will quickly lead to the emergence of a strong foreign-owned sector. By 2000 it will be meeting over 20 per cent of domestic demand in Eastern Europe and its share of exports and imports will undoubtedly be even bigger. Another feature of Eastern Europe worth noting is that, unlike many other parts of the world, there is little popular resistance to foreign investment, the majority of society seeing it as a spur to modernization of economies, acceleration of growth and 'Europeanization'.

This new situation is arousing growing interest among capital exporters in the West. Frightened away at first by muddle, red tape, and inefficient bureaucracies or more mundane inconveniences like scarcity of hotel accommodation, poor telephone services, etc., they soon began to view the new opportunities with greater enthusiasm. This new attitude can be partly attributed to the unexpected pace of developments in Eastern Europe itself where obstacles to more open relations with other countries are being systematically removed. This is a matter not only of changes in regulations and the formation of government agencies charged with attracting foreign investment, but also of such things as rapid improvements in the essential infrastructure (e.g. the opening in the past two years of many new hotels, better international telephone system, more fax machines) and immense advances in the consciousness of the public and in management development. In this last area Eastern Europe owes much to assistance from the West – the British Know-How Fund, for one – and international organizations. In the last three years large numbers of East Europeans have been given opportunities to travel to the West for the purpose of improving their professional skills. Thousands of persons have attended all sorts of courses, business schools, schools of management, etc., sponsored by West European countries and international organizations. Many of them now occupy senior positions in the government departments responsible for smoothing the path of foreign enterprise into Eastern Europe.

The enthusiasm with which foreign investment is regarded by many East European economists does not mean that all obstacles have vanished. There are still many left, some arising from the objective situation in Eastern Europe (in the field of professional staff, for example), others from the fact that Western businessmen tend to have an uncertain grasp of the realities in these countries and their problems of adaptation to the new conditions, though that varies. Germans and Austrians have the best appreciation of the situation, other West Europeans and Americans are less well informed, while for the Japanese, for instance, Eastern Europe is a newly discovered continent. Even studies carried out by large and prestigious West European consultants are full of obvious errors and evaluations that give clear evidence of only the most nodding acquaintance with the actual situation. Without a doubt this problem will also disappear before long, thanks to the keen interest in East European affairs being displayed by Western experts, the research conducted by many centres, the establishment of data banks, and the first-hand experience accumulated by businessmen in the course of direct contacts.

Evaluations of the economic situation in Eastern Europe are impeded by the extreme unreliability of the data available from the national statistical offices, the result largely of the practices of the communist period. Basic information, other than demographic, is now being questioned as more and more comes to light about the methods used to falsify statistics at every level of the elaborate reporting structure of the communist period. Many aggregate values are unknown, even approximately; for instance, no one has yet been able to compute with any degree of accuracy the national product of these countries (in some cases variations in estimates have a range of one to three). Also unknown is the real volume of foreign investment. However, from partial data, such as the number of registered enterprises with partly foreign-held equity, the size of their capital stock, and investment plans approved by government agencies, certain conclusions can be drawn, pending the more complete information which will doubtless start to arrive in two to three years' time.

The subject of this book is foreign investment in Eastern Europe. The term 'foreign enterprise', which occurs passim, is used for convenience to refer to any firm investing in Eastern Europe whose capital is wholly or partly foreign owned. Hitherto much the greater part of the inflow of foreign capital has taken the form of direct investment and that, too, has been the chief focus of interest, though due attention has also been given to indirect investment whose significance will grow swiftly.

The book is divided into seven chapters. The first chapter summarizes the changes taking place in the economies and policies of the seven East European countries with special emphasis on the factors exerting the biggest influence on the scale and possibilities of foreign investment. The second chapter looks at the role of foreign owned enterprises in the process of change as viewed by the societies and governments of the countries concerned and answers the key question: why do East European governments want to attract foreign investment? The third chapter examines the measures employed for this purpose by each country and offers an overview of the evolution of legal regulations relating to foreign investment. The fourth chapter considers the attitude of foreign enterprises to direct investment in Eastern Europe. The fifth and sixth chapters are devoted to the structure of foreign investment (by industry) and its geographical distribution (by country of origin and destination of the capital).

These chapters are all concerned solely with direct investment, until recently the only form practised in Eastern Europe. By direct investment we usually mean the launching of a new enterprise in another country and its subsequent expansion or the purchase of a sufficient quantity of the stock of a foreign enterprise to give the investor a say in its effective management.

The seventh chapter deals with a form of foreign investment new to Eastern Europe. This is portfolio investment which is expected to commence in the majority of the countries of this region in 1991 or 1992 and is likely to grow in importance thereafter. Portfolio investment is here understood as the purchasing of securities and small blocks of shares in enterprises.

The book ends with an analysis of the future for foreign enterprises in Eastern Europe.

To prepare this book I conducted research in all the countries of the region with the exception of Albania and met with economists, managers, and policy-makers. Of great value, too, was the International Small Business Congress in Seoul during which I had the opportunity to talk to a large number of entrepreneurs. In analysing the changes in progress and the legal status I have drawn principally on local sources such as statements by political leaders and other prominent figures, legislation relating to foreign investment and privatization, and statistical yearbooks. Much of the information comes from mimeographed material prepared by agencies, offices, ministries, and academics. However, there is still a gap in the literature in respect of surveys of foreign investments currently in progress in Eastern Europe.

I had no access to the majority of basic Albanian sources. Albania is in fact the country in which change is least visible and foreign investment still next to negligible. Until the end of 1990 this interesting country was still a 'skansen* of communism'. Consequently, a substantial proportion of my general observations about Eastern Europe do not apply to Albania, though there is no question that it, too, has now started out on the path chosen by the rest of Eastern Europe.

* an open-air museum of old constructions, with their equipment

1 Political and economic change in Eastern Europe

There is a direct linkage between the situation in the field of foreign investment and the general political and economic situation in a particular area. If the latter is found disquieting by foreign companies, their usual response is to pull out. Foreign investment is absolutely impossible without the assent of the host governments – and for many years that was not forthcoming. For this reason a brief recapitulation of the changes that have taken place there since the Second World War with special emphasis on the most recent developments is essential.

EAST EUROPEAN COMMUNISM

From the economic point of view Eastern Europe can be divided into two halves: north and south. The first comprises the countries that belong geographically to Central Europe:[1] Poland, Czechoslovakia, Hungary, and northern Yugoslavia (now independent Slovenia and Croatia). Even prior to the First World War these were countries with capitalist systems, large indigenous middle classes, and extensive railway networks. The southern part of the region, comprising the rest of Yugoslavia and the whole of Romania, Bulgaria, and Albania, was much more backward. In these countries industry was very scant, the vast majority of the population lived on the land, the middle class was small, and the infrastructure rudimentary.

Though the communist system reduced to some extent the differences in the region's economic levels, these still remained very appreciable (see Tables 1.1 and 1.2). Among the immense economic and social changes that it effected, the following need to be noted here:

1 Acceleration of industrialization processes. In all the countries of Eastern Europe manufacturing became the strongest sector of the economy. Although for the most part this manufacturing sector is technically backward and has low productivity standards, gross output is

Table 1.1 Area, population, and employment in manufacturing (1989)

	Area '000 km^2	Population			Employment in manufacturing '000,000
Albania	28.7	3.2	2.6	39	–
Bulgaria	111.0	9.4	7.6	67	1.4
Czechoslovakia	127.9	15.6	12.6	76	3.0
Hungary	93.0	10.6	8.6	60	1.5
Poland	312.7	37.9	30.7	61	5.2
Romania	237.5	23.2	18.8	51	4.0
Yugoslavia	255.8	23.7	19.2	47	2.9
Total	1,116.6	123.6	100.0	–	C.18.4

Sources: Rocznik Statystyczny, Warsaw, GUS, 1989, pp. 524, 525; *Monthly Bulletin of Statistics*, 1990, No.5, pp. 1–3.

Note: Employment outside agriculture is for 1987.

Table 1.2 Output of selected products (1988)

	Coal '000,000 tonnes	Electricity '000,000 Kwh	Steel '000,000 tonnes	Cars '000	Tractors '000	TV sets '000
Albania	2.3	–	0.1	–	–	–
Bulgaria	34.1	45.1	2.9	15	4.8	199
Czechoslovakia	123.5	87.1	15.4	164	38.4	503
Hungary	20.9	29.2	3.6	–	–	414
Poland	266.5	144.0	16.9	292	59.5	647
Romania	67.5	75.0	14.3	121	39.2	530
Yugoslavia	60.0	82.5	2.4	310	–	591
Total	574.8	c.463	c.55.6	902	c.142	c.2,885

Sources: Rocznik Statystyczny, Warsaw, GUS, 1989, *passim*; *Monthly Bulletin of Statistics*, 1990, No.5, *passim*.

Note: Coal production includes both hard and brown coal; Romanian tractor output is for 1987.

substantial (especially in heavy industry). The type of industrialization that was put into effect created employment for a huge mass of workers and provided the facilities for acquiring basic vocational skills. For training staff there are several hundred colleges of technology, but the best use is not made of this human capital. The large amount of relatively well-trained manpower is now one of the chief selling points in attracting foreign investment.

2 Slowdown in agricultural development. Agriculture was sacrificed to industry. It is an inefficient sector with, by European standards, low crop yields per hectare and per person employed. As a result East European countries were forced to import growing quantities of farm products, which was a severe strain on their balance of payments and created dependence on the West. That eventually led them to revise their agricultural policies (ensuring, for instance, larger supplies of machinery and higher levels of artificial fertilizer consumption). The potential of East European agriculture as a growth area is very considerable, but only given changes in the structure of both ownership and production.

The communist system was introduced in Eastern Europe in 1944–8 and based on the Soviet model of which at first it was literally an exact carbon copy.[2] For example, the Czechoslovak economists who worked on their country's first development plan received instructions to set targets for reindeer production and construction of ocean-going ships. An extensive model of economic development was put into effect. It consisted in the movement of millions of people from a backward agricultural sector to newly created, though already outdated, industries, and with very limited expenditure on development of the infrastructure. Needless to say, in the early years output grew very quickly, but in due course increasingly powerful brakes inevitably began to be applied. They sprang chiefly from the weakening of agriculture, the skimping on investment in infrastructure, and, first and foremost, the technological backwardness and inefficient organization of industry. In view of what has been learned in recent years about the regular falsification of statistics in Eastern Europe it is impossible to make an accurate estimate of the decline in growth rates, but even the official figures show that it was appreciable. Towards the end of the 1970s all these countries (with the possible exception of Albania whose economic situation is obscure) were overtaken by economic recession for the first time since the war: the fall in production in many crucial areas was so steep that it could no longer be masked by manipulating statistics. The 1980s saw the decline continue, and East European economies slid into a crisis from which they have yet to recover.

The crisis was aggravated by a 'debt trap'. From 1970 onwards Eastern

Europe (again with the exception of Albania) began trying to modernize its economies and raise real living standards through the expedient of borrowing abroad. The calculation was simple: investment projects financed by credits would act as a dynamic impetus to growth and boost export earnings out of which the debts would then be paid. Mismanagement plus a considerable amount of corruption resulted in production rising far more slowly than was expected. Bribery of East European officials by Western companies became a common practice and led, among other things, to the purchase of many items of machinery and equipment that proved totally useless (it has been variously estimated that from 60 to 80 per cent of the capital goods procurement made in the West in the 1970s failed to meet expectation). That being so, credits could not be repaid. It is symptomatic that the biggest debtors are countries whose leaders cultivated closer economic ties with the West (Hungary, Poland, and Yugoslavia), while the ones with the lightest burden are Czechoslovakia, which was denied credits by the West for political reasons, and Albania, which spurned them on ideological grounds. Because of the failure to meet obligations on schedule, the total owed snowballed, and by the late 1980s external debt had become one of the East European economies' most formidable problems (see the Appendix, Table A.5). Together with structural ailments, it has been a major factor in the deepening economic crisis.[3]

Another serious obstacle to development and modernization in Eastern Europe was the channelling of a very high percentage of national income into armaments. These countries maintained Europe's largest tank army and for over forty years accorded absolute priority in the allocation of resources and hard currency to munitions plants. Each built up defence industries beyond the means of backward economies.

The economic crisis that set in at the end of the 1970s inevitably developed into a political crisis. In each country it followed a different course since with the passage of time their economic and political situations had diverged. We have seen that in all seven the policy after the war was to install uniform replicas of the Stalinist system in the USSR. The reaction of the populations varied; copies closest to the original were implemented in Albania, Bulgaria, and Romania. In Poland, Czechoslovakia, and Hungary popular resistance resulted in substantial and eventually increasing deviations from the model (in Poland, for instance, since 1956 about 80 per cent of the land has since 1956 belonged to private farmers). Consequently what we had everywhere were exogenous systems in which there was a problem of the originality of the model. In political terms all these countries were totalitarian states, but it is possible to distinguish a 'soft' and a 'hard' variety (Albania, Bulgaria, and Romania). The 'hard' regimes also included Yugoslavia which at first faithfully copied the Soviet model, but then in

1948 embarked on increasingly radical departures which in due course coagulated into its 'self-management' system.

In each country the totalitarian system developed its own elite which had a vital stake in preserving the status quo. These elites are often identified with the 'Nomenclatura', a term worth elucidating. In communist countries there were two parallel and complementary power apparatuses: state and party, each similarly subdivided functionally (e.g. central committee departments, government ministries) and geographically. All senior and middle-ranking posts in industry and the administration could only be filled by persons approved by the equivalent level echelon of the party structure (e.g. the central committee organization department). It was the people on these lists of names with party clearance who formed the Nomenclatura (which effectively also included employees of the party apparatus). In large industrial establishments all senior managerial appointments were restricted to the Nomenclatura; in smaller enterprises it might be only the managing director. The Nomenclatura was, therefore, a usually pliant tool in the hands of communist party leaders, but composed largely of typical 'organization men', loyal and quiescent, but short on drive and mostly lacking in administrative ability. This system tended, therefore, to produce ruling elites which were none too competent. They were a perfect instrument for upholding and entrenching communist power and implementing party policy in settled periods when things were going relatively well, but were clearly out of their depth when faced with difficulties and political tensions. In times of political crisis the power apparatus in all communist countries went to pieces, and the Nomenclatura's recipe for survival was to keep their heads down and wait for things to even out. In the economic sphere that only served to make a bad situation even worse.

Communist ideology was founded on the dogma of 'dictatorship of the proletariat' which was translated in Eastern Europe as dictatorship of the working class over the rest of society. The corollary, needless to say, was that any kind of cooperation with the 'exploiting classes', least of all with foreign capital, could only be a temporary tactical manoeuvre. Power was wielded in the name of the working class by the communist parties, though with various appellations being used (e.g. 'workers', 'labour', etc.). In the 1950s the majority of the industrial working class in all seven countries consisted of recent immigrants from rural areas and small towns with little or no experience of political activity; among them the communist parties found a large following. Eventually, however, there came about a change within a generation. By the 1970s most of the workers in big enterprises were urban born. The working class, now large in number, relatively well trained but ill-paid, grew increasingly disaffected. Large industrial plants and mining centres became hotbeds of unrest which the authorities sought to quell by a stick-and-carrot mixture of repression and wage increases. The money for such placation of the workers at a time when the economic situation of the East European countries was very strained was first found from more borrowing abroad and when this, too, proved not enough a rapidly worsening budget deficit.

The combination of swiftly rising incomes and only barely growing output inevitably led in the 1980s to a widening gap between supply and demand. That in turn was bound to trigger either inflation with all its negative consequences or market shortages. In Poland, Romania, and Bulgaria both phenomena occurred simultaneously: prices rose more slowly than incomes, which stripped the market of essential goods. For fear of worker revolt governments shrank from increasing prices at the same rate as incomes. As a result an ever larger number of enterprises faced growing deficits, which forced governments to expand the system of subsidies (for both particular producers and particular products), thus further encumbering budgets and creating additional distortions in the price structure.

Within each East European country there were communist functionaries who realized that the system was doomed. Their reaction was simple: salvage as much as possible from the sinking ship and keep what they could for themselves. Some were satisfied with villas and with money. Others decided to help themselves to some of the capital assets they had managed and administered, and became entrepreneurs on their own behalf. As a result the end of the 1980s saw the eruption in Hungary and Poland, and to a lesser extent in other East European countries as well (though not Albania), of a rash of what have been dubbed 'Nomenclatura companies'. These are vehicles for the appropriation by high-ranking bureaucrats and politicians (often using relatives as nominees) of a growing slice of national income. The method most often used was for the partners in such a venture to lease for a nominal sum the most profitable departments of an enterprise under their control and bank on the gradual conversion of the company so formed into a normal private firm of the capitalist type. Many members of the Nomenclatura were less ambitious, as in the case of a recent Polish foreign minister, for example, who simply acquired a multi-storey building in Warsaw with a large pharmacy on the ground floor.

What happened, therefore, was a speeding-up in the decomposition of communism with some of the pillars of its establishment acquiring a personal stake in the conversion of the existing system into a capitalist one. Previously (until the end of the 1970s) the way to halt the slide would have been Soviet military intervention. In the 1980s, however, rapid economic and political disintegration overtook the USSR itself, isolationist tendencies began to deepen, and control of the state passed into increasingly reform-oriented hands. The new Soviet leaders, their faith in communist dogma evaporating, ceased to be interested in propping up communist regimes in neighbouring countries as that was a threat to their policies. The shifts in Soviet policy unquestionably spurred change that no doubt would otherwise have taken longer.

In Hungary, Poland, and Yugoslavia leadership of the communist party was assumed by politicians who, recognizing that a change of system was inevitable, gradually came to see that their only option was to preside over that process themselves; in other words, to try and change the economic system, but at the same time ensure that the party retained its dominant position. That was the point of the reforms undertaken by Grosz in Hungary and Messner and Rakowski in Poland. All sectors of the economy were, in theory at least, put on an equal footing, which meant that the private sector was accorded the same rights as those enjoyed by the hitherto privileged 'social property' (i.e., state-owned and cooperative) sector. The administrative procedures for licensing private enterprise were simplified, and it was allowed into areas from which it had once been barred (such as insurance or wholesaling). New regulations were introduced which offered a better deal for foreign investors.

In the political field the aim was to disarm the opposition by granting certain basic civil rights. Most detained opposition activists were released; prosecution of people taking part in 'unlawful assemblies' and political demonstrations ceased; and talks with the principal opposition forces started. Schemes for 'national entente' were proposed by the communists under which, at the cost of some opposition representation in government, they could hope to keep a grip for many years to come on the armed forces and police and hold the key office of president. The first country in which agreement was reached was Poland – as a result of negotiations ('Round Table') which lasted from 6 February to 4 April 1989. With these accords concluded, the reformers thought they had the situation under control. However, there was one crucial contingency for which they had not bargained: the collapse of communist parties from within. Divested of their privileges, members of the Polish United Workers Party began saying the same things as the rest of society. A party over 2 million strong became a spent force.

Seeing the wind of change, many senior officials and even some members of the military establishment began voicing 'new' views. The situation slid out of the communists' hands. Deserted by their own party faithful and reduced to a minority in parliament, the communists were driven out of one position after another. Let us recall the landmark dates: 3 June 1989: landslide defeat in 'semi-democratic' parliamentary election; 15 August: instalment of opposition leader Tadeusz Mazowiecki as Prime

Minister; April 1990: surrender of the defence and interior ministries to non-communists. In January 1990 the communist party itself ceased to exist. Some of its members organized small successor parties; most decided to become private citizens getting on with their own lives – and in many cases, businesses. The former communist Minister of Industry, Mieczyslaw Wilczek, already a millionaire in 1989, became a billionaire setting up a string of new enterprises, and there were hundreds of others like him. The new government formed in September 1989 lost no time in setting about dismantling the old system and moving closer and closer towards a free-market economy and capitalist system.

Poland's example was quickly followed by other East European nations. In Hungary that was easy: communist reformers had already erected some of the scaffolding for the construction of capitalism. Acceleration of change began in September 1989 and the victory of the Democratic Forum (MDF) in the general election on 8 April 1990 set the seal on the transfer of power to the former opposition. In Czechoslovakia hard-line party leaders tried to hang on by force (e.g. violent suppression of the demonstration in Prague on 17 November 1989), but in the end were compelled to step down, largely by the threat of a general strike; on 7 December a government was formed in which the majority of posts went to one-time opposition members, on 29 December Vaclav Havel, months earlier still a hounded dissident, was elected President, and the defeat of the communist party at the polls on 8–9 June 1990 dealt the quietus to the old regime.

In Yugoslavia the situation is far more complicated. It is a federation whose cohesion was ensured by a communist-controlled army. The party itself, the League of Communists, racked by fierce faction-fighting, fell apart when nationality conflicts compounded the political quarrels. In 1988–90 the central government carried out economic reforms which intro-duced many capitalist elements. In the political sphere, with the system crumbling, opposition forces were allowed an increasing degree of free-dom, which eventually resulted in election victories for local opposition parties in Slovenia (22 April 1990) and Croatia (6 May), and subsequently in Bosnia-Herzegovina and Macedonia; in Serbia and Montenegro power has been retained by former communists. In 1991 Slovenia, Croatia and Macedonia proclaimed independence, which started a devastating civil war.

In Romania changes took yet another form. After bloodily suppressing the first wave of popular revolt, the communist regime of Nicolai Ceausescu was finally overthrown on 22 December 1989. Power was assumed by a National Salvation Front headed by politicians with varying backgrounds but including many former communists. The communist party ceased to exist. In the election on 20 May 1990 the Front and its leader, Ion

Iliescu, defeated its out-and-out anti-communist rivals. Iliescu is pursuing a policy of slow and cautious change aimed at modernization of Romania but without upheavals.[4]

A similar policy of gradual change has been embraced by the Bulgarian government which was until recently dominated by communists of a reformist persuasion. The general election on 13 October 1991 gave a majority to anti-communist parties and in November 1991 a government of the Union of Democratic Forces was created. In both Romania and Bulgaria the downfall of the communist system is inevitable. The thrust of government policy is towards building up capitalist elements, but there is inconsistency in its implementation, slowing down the pace of change.

The only East European country in which communists have retained total control until mid-1991, though after abandoning some of their fundamental ideological tenets, was Albania. A flurry of demonstrations and the flight of a small number of Albanians to take refuge in foreign embassies in 1990 came as a shock to a country in which the communist regime seemed impregnable, but was not enough to shake the basic fabric of the system. In July 1990 there came the first signs of major changes: dismissal of the most conservative leaders (including the defence and security ministers) and government acceptance of private retailing and services. In December 1990 the government accepted a multi-party system and the principle of free elections, and finally in June 1991 the first non-communist-dominated government was created.

Summing up, we can say that in all the seven East European countries the following changes have taken place in the 1989–91 period:

1 democratization, freedom of political organization, and the first free elections in over forty years;
2 weakening or dissolution of communist parties, removal from power of much of the Nomenclatura and their replacement by former opposition activists or, more rarely, apolitical experts;
3 commencement of progress towards free-market economies of a capitalist type.

These changes have produced a qualitatively new situation for foreign business opening up opportunities for foreign investment on a scale many times greater than in the past.

PRIVATE SECTOR

For foreign investors a crucial question is the ownership structure in a given country. It is one thing if firms' dealings are restricted to state enterprises, quite another if they can also do business with the private sector. In this respect, even prior to 1989, the situation in Eastern Europe varied from country to country. In theory the regimes in all seven were committed to abolishing 'the exploitation of man by man' which presupposed the expropriation of all private employers of paid labour. Though communist dogma did in fact tolerate the existence of family businesses, agricultural small holdings, and so on, it regarded them as less productive than large 'socialist' enterprises and so doomed to disappear. In actual practice things were different. In Hungary, Poland, and Yugoslavia there was a largish private sector consisting of most craft workshops, part of the services and retailing network, some low-stream industry, and, in Poland and Yugoslavia, a majority of individual land holdings (in Poland 76 per cent of arable land in 1988 belonged to private farmers who accounted for no less than 86 per cent of the value added of agriculture).[5] In Czechoslovakia, Romania, and Bulgaria the private sector was much smaller; in 1989 it comprised a small proportion of shops and service establishments and in agriculture the very small plots of land adjoining cooperative and state farm workers' dwellings). In Albania all means of production were treated as 'social property' (state-owned or cooperative), and there was no officially registered private sector.

In all East European countries, Albania included, there was also a thriving unofficial economy consisting of services (e.g. car repairs or house construction), retailing, and even production (e.g. clothing). In Hungary attempts were made to legalize this sector. The government began issuing permits for various kinds of after-hours jobs and even in some cases the use for these purposes of machinery in state-owned factories. There arose what was called an 'employees' complementary sector' (see Table 1.3) comprising a growing part of the unofficial economy. In the course of the 1980s the role of the unofficial sector in East European economies grew. In the atmosphere generated by the decomposition of communism speculation, often in the form of using public property for private profit, became rife.

Table 1.3 National income in Hungary according to different forms of property (in per cent)

Type of property	1970	1980	1990
Socialist sector	94.3	92.8	86.4
Employees' complementary sector	3.1	3.7	6.6
Private sector	2.6	3.5	7.0

Source: *Statistical Almanac*, Budapest, Statistical Office of Hungary, 1981 and 1990.

The fattest profits lay in building plots, apartments, and foreign merchandise. There was a boom in smuggling – to which, for that matter, the authorities (except in Albania) virtually turned a blind eye. At first it involved movement of goods between the East European countries themselves and, no less lucrative, to and from the USSR. In view of the scale of the phenomenon and most governments' disinterested attitudes it seems more appropriate to talk of foreign trade than smuggling. In due course the practice was extended to trading in Western goods.

It is estimated that in 1990 trafficking in foreign merchandise was the staple livelihood of over a million East Europeans and a sideline for another million. Given the general low levels of pay, a Hungarian, for instance, could, by topping up the modest official travel allowance with currency bought on the black market, earn more from a couple of shopping trips to nearby Vienna for electronic goods than the annual income from a relatively well-paid government job. Before long there was a group of big-time dealers – effectively businessmen – who had accumulated the means to start importing in bulk (into Poland, Hungary, Yugoslavia, often in whole container loads). Some idea of the dimensions of this unofficial trade can be gained from the volume of purchases in particular countries. For instance, it is estimated that in 1987 Poles took at least 300 million dollars' worth of merchandise (80 per cent of it clothing, mainly denim) out of Turkey. 'Unofficial traders' from Eastern Europe annually spend over 200 million dollars in the foreign-trade zones of the United Arab Emirates. Bigger still, though harder to estimate, is the flow of goods from Berlin and Vienna. For over ten years this has been a business bringing in immense profits.

The growth of the unofficial economy led to the emergence in Eastern Europe of a class of resourceful entrepreneurs with large funds at their disposal and in many cases their own domestic sales networks. They are particularly numerous in Poland, Yugoslavia, and Hungary. But even in Czechoslovakia where profiteering, smuggling, and private trade were until 1989 fiercely suppressed by the communist authorities, there arose a sizeable group of millionaires. In that category the Czechoslovak Union of Private Businessmen places persons with a net worth exceeding 10 million krone, a very substantial sum in that country, and puts their number at over 50,000.

The new non-communist governments face the difficult problem of how to harness this huge quantity of speculative capital to productive use and persuade speculators, unlicenced traders, and the like to open normal, officially registered businesses.

In the first few months the contrary happened. The atrophy of the old administration, the muddle caused by changes in thousands of regulations, and a general disregard of laws frequently regarded as absurd made for an even more rapid growth of the unofficial economy. The streets and squares of Eastern Europe (still with the exception of Albania) filled up with tens of thousands of traders, some of them operating on a large scale. Some unofficial distributors resell to dozens of stall holders and have their own fleets of delivery trucks. The profits reaped from these operations are estimated in billions of dollars.

A remedy for this situation is being sought in reform of the tax system. The introduction in some countries of general income tax will make it possible for the first time since the Second World War for governments to pursue a policy of controlling speculation by discouraging certain kinds of activity through high taxes and offering incentives to others. This has been instrumental in the decisions of a large number of traders to turn what have been illegal operations into normal, registered enterprises.

In Poland the government, at the same time as making the zloty internally convertible, also permitted the opening of private bureaux de change, and advantage was taken of this opportunity by several thousand currency dealers, many of them previously involved in the black market. A growing stream of imports is now handled by officially registered private firms whose proprietors are one-time 'smuggling barons' who can now do business legitimately under the new laws. Similar, if slower, developments can be observed in Hungary and are likely before long to spread to other East European countries (which in 1990 faced similar mounting tides of speculation and illegal dealings).

We often read in publications about Eastern Europe that progress in systemic transformation will be exceedingly slow on account of the lack of investment funds. That is only partly true since it fails to allow for this process of 'primitive accumulation of capital', much of it of illegal origin. From the moral point of view it is not, of course, unequivocally indefensible – any more than another of its characteristics: the illegal labour of East Europeans in Western Europe and North America. In 1988–9 over a million and in 1990 1.5 million travelled abroad to work as often as not contrary to the regulations of the host country (official employment is restricted to a certain quota of Yugoslavs and a very small number of persons from other East European countries). The money put aside from jobs in the West, often multiplied by profitable commercial transactions, has provided the capital for many private business projects. For example, near Zadar (Croatia) I met the owner of a campsite who had previously worked illegally in Austria. There, out of his savings, he bought some secondhand trucks which he then sold, and from the proceeds built and equipped his campsite and later a small meat-packing plant. He now owns a slaughterhouse and deals in trucks and land.

Poland, Czechoslovakia, and Hungary have already introduced

legislation similar to that in force in Western Europe (in Czechoslovakia and Hungary modelled largely on the Austrian system) which has led to an incredibly rapid proliferation of private firms. In just two years many of these small businesses have grown into large enterprises; among them are banks, industrial plants, and private department stores.

It is interesting that this dynamic growth of private firms has come at a time when East European governments are trying to solve their financial difficulties by means of tax squeezes. In Hungary and Poland high taxation has badly hit some of the traditional service fields (e.g. shoe repairs) and even small-scale industry (e.g. production of many building materials). Another highly damaging blow to the private sector was dealt by acute recession. In all East European countries the fall of communism had the effect of an abrupt downturn in the economy. To a large extent it was due to the new governments' efforts to create conditions for pressing on with economic reform and speeding up structural change. One of the basic prerequisites of movement towards a free-market system was the overhaul of the price structure and equalization of supply and demand. Bringing supply into balance with a far greater aggregate demand was bound in itself, with the dismantlement of the centralized system, to cause a steep rise in prices. Their restructuring was a second inflationary factor: predictably, what had been inordinately underpriced goods were bid up sharply, while the overpriced remained as they were. The third principal spur to inflation came from the pay awards secured by some occupational groups.

The most radical pace of change was set in Poland where price controls were rapidly scrapped; there, too, in 1989 and at the beginning of 1990 inflation was highest. After several months of dizzily climbing prices a demand barrier appeared: people reduced their purchases of many goods. At the same time a flow of imported merchandise produced greater competition. Together, this resulted in mid-1990 in an abrupt drop in inflation, stabilization of the market situation through a plentiful supply of goods, and far sounder price relationships than at any time in the preceding forty years. In Hungary attempts to rationalize prices had started earlier and inflation in 1989–90 was slower, but even so in mid-1991 the rate was still high. Inflation reached its most galloping proportions in Yugoslavia where prices rose tens of times over 1987–9; reforms implemented by the government of Prime Minister Markovic led to a temporary stabilization of the new dinar by October 1990. In Czechoslovakia, Romania, and Bulgaria, on the other hand, reforms sent inflation soaring in 1990, and the market situation in these countries deteriorated.

Another effect of the changes in the price system in Eastern Europe and the wider opening of the door to imports was the discovery that the production of many articles cost too much and was often unnecessary. In other words, the viability of the structure of production began to be tested by the market. In industries in which this happened quickly there followed a sharp drop in demand and so also in output. Recession became more acute in Poland where, despite a growth in exports, gross domestic product declined over 1990 by no less than 20 per cent. Lay-offs of workers began and for the first time in over forty years the spectre of unemployment reared its head. Similar developments, though on a smaller scale, occurred in Hungary and towards the end of 1990 also started to surface in all the other East European countries with the exception of Albania. In Yugoslavia, since the self-management system had much earlier made for a better price and production structure than elsewhere and unemployment was earlier a permanent feature of economic life, the changes carried out in 1990 were less significant.

THE PRIVATIZATION PROCESS

The restructuring of prices made it possible to embark on longer-term structural changes; among these special attention needs to be given to privatization. In countries in which the state controlled over 85 per cent of production and in some (Romania, Bulgaria) even 90 per cent, this is of fundamental importance and needs to be planned on a scale many times greater than the privatization undertaken in the 1980s in, for instance, Britain or France.

Privatization processes in Eastern Europe are commonly divided into 'small-scale' and 'large-scale' privatization. The former comprises the transfer to private ownership of small state-owned or cooperative enterprises (mainly in the field of trade and other services), premises, and land. Small-scale privatization had in fact begun in all these countries under the old communist regimes (even in Albania in July 1990). It is a difficult process on account of the great number of establishments to be privatized, the complex problem of ownership, and the meagerness of savings accumulated by employees of the shops and other enterprises involved (since it is they who are usually envisaged as the new owners).

In Hungary the number of private shop and restaurant proprietors rose in 1981–9 from 15,000 to 40,000, but their share of the retailing and catering trade came to only 13 per cent.[6] The dominant position was still occupied by establishments owned by the state or government-controlled cooperatives. About 4,000 of these were spontaneously privatized in 1989 and 1990 (largely through conversion into small limited liability companies). That left over 49,000 state and cooperative firms. Some of these are now being privatized under Law LXXIV/1990, and the process is to be completed in 1992.

In Czechoslovakia regulations instituting privatization of small estab-lishments were issued on 25 October 1990 and provide for the transfer to private ownership of almost 100,000 stores, hotels, repair shops, and bakeries. The process of small-scale privatization got under way in January 1991 and is being effected largely through auctions organized by local authorities. In the first round only Czechoslovak nationals and enterprises can take part; in the second the bidding is also opened to foreign buyers.

In Bulgaria, Romania, and Albania small-scale privatization is pro-ceeding relatively slowly. In mid-1991 the state and the large cooperative organizations still controlled over 70 per cent of the trade. Nevertheless, there can be no doubt that the process will continue to go forward.

The greatest difficulties were encountered in Poland on account of the very large number of state and para-statal cooperative establishments (over 110,000), the fact that most of them were cooperative property, and queries over the ownership of premises (in many cases located in buildings also in the process of privatization).[7] By November 1991 over 90 per cent of shops had passed into private hands.

It is harder to give figures for the growth of the private sector through new capital formation. Official statistics classify all registered businesses as enter-prises, including even stall holders under that heading. In October 1990 there were 270,000 such businesses in Hungary and 990,054 in Poland.[8] In the latter country some 200,000 of these were firms employing not only their proprietors' families but also paid staff and with plans for expanding further. Only a few hundred had actually succeeded in doing so by the end of 1991 and turned their owners into big entrepreneurs with millions of dollars of dis-posable capital. A large number of these have entered into partnerships with foreign investors (for instance, through participation in joint ventures).

Small-scale privatization processes are gradually changing the situation in the exchange of goods and services, demonopolizing trade and sub-jecting it to free-market rules. For foreign enterprises this is also an impor-tant development since it means that they have the same access to the new private firms as other suppliers (previously enterprises in the public sector enjoyed privileged treatment). Now their competitiveness depends solely on price and quality. In the services sector privatization is proving a blessing, for foreign investors are benefiting: in some areas the quality of the services offered by local firms has improved, so increasing competition on the market.

The concept of large-scale privatization has in practice two different meanings:

1 reconstitution of public enterprises as registered private enterprises (some of these become 'companies' in which the sole stockholder is the state);

2   total or partial transfer to private ownership of large public enterprises (in industry, transport, construction, banking, insurance, wholesaling, etc.).

Only the second of these definitions seems to cover privatization properly.

In the case of large-scale privatization the difficulties involved are augmented by the lopsided structure of East European economies. In 1989 large enterprises accounted for almost 80 per cent of the national product in these countries.

Privatization of large public enterprises is now being pursued on a broad scale in Poland and Hungary, and in 1990 also started in the other countries of the region, again with the exception of Albania. A whole series of conditions have to be fulfilled if such privatization is to yield the desired results. First and foremost, there has to be a class of entrepreneurs capable of dynamic leadership of large operations and possessing substantial capital resources. There is, of course, no lack of people with drive and initiative in Eastern Europe; the basic problem is that the majority of them do not have the necessary funds or management experience. As we have noted, an accelerated process of 'primitive capital accumulation' took place in Poland, Hungary, and Yugoslavia which has produced a relatively large group of local entrepreneurs in each. These people must now not only be encouraged to change the way they do business but also have to learn the fundamental rules of capitalist economics and enterprise management. Being for the most part young, go-ahead and intelligent, they would profit greatly from the assistance that Western countries can provide in this field.

Needless to say, these 'primitive accumulation' processes have not created stocks of private capital in Eastern Europe large enough to make possible immediate takeovers of the majority of public enterprises. Though there are no reliable estimates of the size of the funds available, it is beyond doubt that they are several times smaller than the real value of all the enterprises to be privatized. The selling-off of state property to private owners (national or foreign) is further complicated by the controversial nature of all the possible methods of appraising the worth of an enterprise's assets. Use of the British criterion of book value standard leads to patent overvaluation. This is due to the kind of investment projects that were carried out in Eastern Europe: in most cases over half their value consisted of the outlays on construction of the buildings and infrastructure, while the share of plant and machinery was very small. Since this lowers enterprises' long-term rates of return, they have to be offered at prices much lower than their book value, which naturally arouses certain objections. The technicalities alone of valuation are very difficult, but nevertheless a large number of Western auditing and consulting firms have come to perform this task according to West European criteria. In Poland and Hungary a number of large Western business consultants have opened branch offices.

Privatization of large enterprises was launched in Eastern Europe without any prior amendments to the existing regulations. However, the vast scope of the changes in progress and a variety of legal problems made it clear that new legislation was needed. In Hungary a string of bills was passed (Law VI/1988, Law V/1990, Law LXXIV/1990, Decree XX/1990, Law VIII/1990) and under their provisions enterprises representing between 5 and 8 per cent of the fixed assets of the whole public sector had been privatized by October 1990.[9] The initial regulations left loopholes for numerous abuses. The criticism they drew, especially in the run-up to the parliamentary election, led to many changes being made, among them Law VI/1990 which set up a State Property Agency to oversee the privatization process. A Programme of National Renewal unveiled by the Hungarian government in September 1990 projects the privatization over the next three to five years of about 50 per cent of state-owned assets (some of them to be acquired by foreign investors).

In Poland Eastern Europe's first comprehensive package of privatization legislation was passed in July 1990.[10] It divides the capital stock of enterprises to be privatized into two issues:

1 20 per cent for sale to their work-forces on very favourable terms (50 per cent of the market value, these shares being subsequently tradeable);
2 80 per cent offered for normal public subscription.[11]

At a ball-park estimate private owners of capital in Poland have the means to acquire 10 to 15 per cent of the equity of privatized enterprises. Since they cannot be expected to commit the whole of their resources to such investment, it is reasonable to suppose they will buy less. So to speed up the privatization process a scheme for free distribution to the whole adult population of vouchers subsequently convertible into shares has been mooted. Some equity is also assigned to social insurance and banking institutions. Shares may also be bought by foreign investors (see chapter 7).

At the end of 1990 legislation was passed which laid down rules for securities trading, organization of stock exchanges, etc. The process of large-scale privatization is supervised by a Ministry of Ownership Changes. About 400 large and medium-sized public enterprises accounting for about 10 per cent of industrial output were sold off by December 1991. It is expected that by 1993 over half of the production in Poland will have passed out of state control and into other ownership sectors.

In Romania, Bulgaria, and Albania large-scale privatization is in its infancy. The situation in Albania at the end of 1991 was that the government was still unable to transfer to private ownership of any large enterprises while in Bulgaria the new regulations were far from clear and in Romania kept changes within specified bounds. In this last country the relevant legislation, adopted on 31 July 1990, provides for the privatization initially of up to 30 per cent of the capital of large enterprises and supervision of this process by a National Privatization Agency. Since the private sector in Romania is not very substantial, all adult citizens will be issued three vouchers each for which they can acquire shares in enterprises of their choice. At a later date a further 45 per cent will be put on the market, with the state retaining the remaining 25 per cent of the stock. The law also permits the leasing to individuals or institutions of enterprises selected by the administration and put out to tender (awarded, presumably, to the highest bidder).[12] The introduction of the new regulations has so far resulted in the leasing of a quickly increasing number of small and medium enterprises by private agents and the acquisition by Romanian citizens of minority holdings in some of the larger enterprises. A significant spur to privatization could come from the creation of opportunities for Romanian and foreign enterprises to form mixed companies, including joint ventures in which private capital (Romanian or external) would in most cases hold a majority of the shares. However, the practical implementation of these provisions is slow.

In Czechoslovakia the key role in the current initial stage of privatization is played by the voucher system. A large proportion of enterprise assets are being transferred to the whole of the public at nominal prices (through distribution of vouchers convertible into shares).[13]

We can sum up by saying that privatization processes are under way in all East European countries, but at a very uneven pace. Table 1.4 ranks them according to their degree of progress along this route.

Table 1.4 Ranking of privatization in Eastern Europe

End-1988	*Mid-1991*
1. Hungary	1. Poland
2. Poland	2. Hungary
3. Yugoslavia	3. Yugoslavia
4. Bulgaria	4. Czechoslovakia
Other countries – effectively no privatization	5. Bulgaria
	6. Romania
	7. Albania

Both the successes and stumbling blocks in privatization can be attributed only in part to objective factors (technical difficulties, scarcity of capital, private entrepreneurs' lack of experience). Of crucial significance is a basic political factor: there is a general realization that privatization holds the key to the burial of all traces of the communist system and the emergence of a fully fledged free-market economy. Consequently, those who believe in a clean sweep are now urging acceleration of privatization and the diehards are doing everything in their power to slow down the process. In each East European country there have also appeared proponents of a 'third way', usually presented as a synthesis of both systems.[14] But the concept is so vague that its advocates have been unable to attract a wide following anywhere.

Between privatization processes and foreign capital flows there is a feedback relationship in Eastern Europe. Foreign investment imparts greater momentum to privatization processes and deepens the consequent changes, while privatization creates normal conditions for the operation of foreign enterprises. Small wonder then that they are drawn chiefly to countries in which privatization processes have gone furthest, are very cautious in their approach to investment in Bulgaria and Romania, and show scant interest in Albania. Before long the rapid changes now taking place will undoubtedly include the latter three countries.

2 East European expectations of foreign investment

RECENT HISTORY

Up to the First World War foreign investment was a very conspicuous feature of the economies of all the countries of Eastern Europe. Of course, in countries as backward as Albania or Bulgaria it reached only a fraction of the scale in what is now Czechoslovakia or Poland. Foreign-owned assets were very extensive, embracing a large part of manufacturing industry and over half of mining production, and also occupying an important place in transport. They were less prominent in trade (dominated by the national minorities of these countries) and next to negligible in agriculture. By law foreign investors nominally had the same status as indigenous investors, local registration of their holdings usually being the only requirement. So, though in many branches of the economy the public administration often subjected foreign enterprises to various forms of discrimination, these were unlawful practices resorted to for the protection of specific interests; for instance, in the areas of Poland occupied by Germany barriers were erected to the investment of capital from other countries in the coal industry. But for the most part foreign investment was regarded as a positive factor and was supported as such, and no restrictions were placed on the transfer of profits.

In the period between the First and Second World Wars the old liberal regulations relating to foreign investment were replaced by new and more detailed provisions aimed at placing foreign-owned property under national control. In many fields the opportunities for foreign capital investment were circumscribed as governments set out to build up their countries' own corporate community. These policies brought the desired results everywhere except Albania and a part of foreign-owned property was gradually taken over by indigenous entrepreneurs. Dammed by the new situation, the stream of foreign capital shrank considerably. Throughout Eastern Europe the outflow of profits transferred by foreign enterprises exceeded the inflow of new capital, which naturally strengthened tendencies to curtail their operations. One of the means employed was compulsory purchase of enterprises involved in certain branches of the economy (e.g. transport). Nevertheless, on the eve of the Second World War foreign enterprises still controlled a significant part of East European economies. In such industries as oil, chemicals, and engineering they accounted for over half of output.

The Second World War brought another major change in the situation of foreign enterprises in Eastern Europe. All of its countries came under direct or indirect German control. The consequences for the foreign ownership sector were sweeping. The majority of firms belonging to enterprises in other countries were expropriated and assigned to German companies. Next, following the liberation of the East European countries, German property was placed under state control which resulted in almost all the existing foreign ownership sector passing 'temporarily' into government hands. The nationalization of the basic factors of production which took place in these countries in 1944–50 clinched the takeover of foreign property by the communist governments. By 1950 throughout Eastern Europe the foreign ownership sector had to all intents and purposes ceased to exist.

For foreign enterprises to own property and factors of production was judged by East European governments to be against the law and 'the socialist social order'. In fact, from a strictly legal point of view the situation in all these countries was more complex: technically, most of the pre-war statutes and regulations remained in force, and these clearly permitted economic activity by foreign entities. Effectively, however, what counted were the post-war laws and, above all, ordinances which were aimed at undermining the sectors of the economy not controlled by the state. A typical feature of communist countries was that law enacted by the legislative power came second to 'mimeograph law', which was the name given to the vast quantity of rule-making material, such as decrees, regulations, directions, and the like, originating in government departments and other central agencies, much of it unconstitutional. For instance, instructions forbidding foreign enterprises to own buildings and machinery were issued in contravention of the law, though this did not prevent courts from dismissing complaints against the bureaucracy's enforcement of them. In political propaganda foreign investment was presented as an activity hostile to the national interest, creating dependence on other countries, and pumping hard currency out of the country.

In the 1960s this stereotype remained binding. However, communist governments began to see that there might be certain advantages in foreign investment, and it gradually became accepted that foreign enterprises could help them to deal with certain marginal, but troublesome, problems. The leaders of most East European countries came to the conclusion that it would pay to create conditions for some kinds of investment projects, but with the proviso that this would not involve any amendments to the legal rules in force or lead to the emergence of a permanent foreign ownership sector. The first step was to allow certain Western service enterprises (e.g. airlines) to set up local offices. The second, and much more important, decision provided for participation in the hotel business and tourism.

In communist countries the tourist trade was chiefly the domain of state tourist offices which concluded contracts with travel agencies in other countries. A major problem was construction of hotel accommodation for foreign visitors, which required both substantial funds and special skills. Even equipping hotels with some of the necessary amenities (e.g. efficient air-conditioning) presented difficulties. The upshot was the conclusion of extremely complicated contracts with Western firms under which they undertook to build hotels, but without ownership rights. In the 1970s the first large, modern hotels began to open in all the East European countries save Albania.

A clause in all these contracts stipulated that the sole owner of the hotel was a national enterprise (usually a state tourist office); the bulk of the construction costs was, however, borne by the Western contractor. On completion the hotel was administered for a specified period (e.g. ten years) by a joint management in which the key posts were usually filled by the foreign investor's representatives. Earnings were shared on an agreed pro rata basis, a large portion being transferred abroad. The foreign investor was also paid a specified fee in hard currency in respect of administration of the hotel and various other services. Since hotel accommodation in the communist countries was very scarce, the new hotels quickly brought in large profits, and the whole operation was a financial winner for both the foreign enterprises and the governments involved. This smoothed the way to the subsequent introduction of new regulations relating to foreign investment.

East European governments found this model of cooperation with foreign business to their liking and tried to extend it to other areas of the economy. But, a few isolated instances apart, that proved impossible. In the case of hotel projects investors could reasonably bank on a relatively rapid recoupment of outlays (three to five years) and satisfactory profits since foreign tourists paid in hard currency, which facilitated a solution to the profit-transfer problem. Elsewhere the financial risk to the investor was much greater, the recoupment period hard to predict, and remittance of profits an awkward stumbling block. Meanwhile East European governments had become aware, however belatedly, of the technological gap separating East and West European industry. Since technology transfer on a basis similar to the hotel construction arrangements was found to be out of the question and 'normal' investment by foreign enterprises was precluded by both regulations and ideology, other possibilities began to be explored.

In the services sector, for all practical purposes this came to nothing, but in the crucial field of manufacturing industry it was decided that modern Western technologies could be secured through co-production schemes. The idea was for hand-picked East European enterprises to enter into participation deals with companies in the West. To this end several thousand contracts, highly complex in their provisions (and often preceded by appropriate international agreements), were negotiated between particular enterprises. The peak period for such deals was 1970–8. A typical example was a contract for the production of tape recorders concluded by the M. Kasprzak Works in Poland with Grundig of West Germany. Under its terms the Polish enterprise obtained a licence, technical assistance in getting the process on stream, machinery, and some components. Payment came out of subsequent deliveries of the finished product to Germany. There was, therefore, a transfer of technology that led to a modernization of production, but the costs of which were borne by the Western side.

In most cases these contracts were implemented by means of Western government or government-guaranteed credits. It was expected that the modernization of production would easily create the means for the repayment of these credits and that this form of cooperation would be expanded. However, it soon became apparent that co-production was for both sides more of a liability than a blessing. With a few exceptions (such as Fiat of Italy) Western companies saw these contracts chiefly as a windfall export opportunity financed by government credits, but were not persuaded that there was anything to be gained from long-term ties. The costs of the operation were for the most part borne by banks and governments, and the credits were of course chargeable to the East European countries. For their part, the majority of East European enterprises proved incapable of choosing the right technologies and making economically profitable use of them. According to various estimates, from 60 to 80 per cent of the Western licences purchased were never put into effect, and a large percentage of the processes actually introduced turned out to be economic liabilities. To this day there is still debate over who was to blame: the Western companies (payment of kickbacks to communist officials in return for purchases of unnecessary capital equipment), the East European enterprises (whose ill-prepared managers concluded disadvantageous contracts and were often unable to discharge the obligations incurred), the state apparatus in these countries, or the general world economic situation? Be that as it may, the principal effect was to drag the East European countries into an increasingly inextricable 'debt trap' (see the Appendix, Table A.5).

Towards the end of the 1970s it became clear to the governments of all these countries that co-production as practised hitherto could not deliver the hoped-for benefits. Meanwhile the technological divide between East and West had continued to widen. This persuaded some communist leaders to rethink their attitude to foreign investment. They concluded that the dogmatic rejection of a foreign ownership sector would have to be abandoned and possibilities had to be created for normal foreign capital investment inclusive of ownership rights. A debate on this subject began in the councils of all communist parties. All these countries decided to change the regulations and allow foreign direct investment, at any rate in some areas of the economy. On the other hand, the opponents of foreign investment found ways of blocking entry to foreign enterprises, usually by taking advantage of contradictory regulations. This was an additional obstacle to attracting foreign investment.

Consequently, each East European country entered a transition period in which foreign investment was permitted, but impeded by various regulations and practices. The pioneer was Romania which opened the door to foreign direct investment as early as 1971; subsequently similar regulations were gradually introduced in other countries. The effective results of this new policy were very meager for reasons which will be analysed in later chapters. The number of large foreign companies operating in Eastern Europe was small in the early years and even as late as 1988 their total investments in all seven countries still fell short of the billion dollar mark. One critical barrier was Western companies' natural suspicion of communist governments and fears of new switches of political course, but a significant role was also played by bad regulations, inefficient bureaucracies, and various objective difficulties. The latter usually sprang from the enclave nature of foreign enterprises which were in effect islands of market mechanisms enclosed within a territory with an economy directly controlled by the state.

Change could only come with abandonment of the communist system and a movement towards 'marketization' of the whole economy. That in fact happened, and the overthrow of the communist system precipitated an abrupt increase in foreign enterprises' interest in capital investment in Eastern Europe. At the same time, there was also a change in the attitude of its governments. It was quickly recognized that foreign investment could play a key role in the process of systemic transformation and foreign enterprises ceased to be viewed as alien enclaves supplying a little hard currency and offering a remedy for minor, if troublesome, ailments. They were now seen as one of the future driving forces of economic development.

THE PRESENT ATTITUDE OF GOVERNMENTS AND PUBLIC OPINION TO FOREIGN INVESTMENT

Following the shift in Albania's position in 1990, there can be no question that the governments of all the countries of Eastern Europe are now decidedly in favour of attracting foreign investment. During their travels to the West, leading politicians are making statements intended to attract investors; for example, the Polish President Lech Walesa said:

> As for Poland, we need foreign investment because it also gives us security. Having a Frenchman or an Englishman here with his factory is like having a division of troops. You in the West have over-production. You can make money out of our shortages and our stupidity – and we have plenty of that.[1]

In official statements growth of foreign investment is presented as one of the most important tasks of the immediate future. The belief in the benefits to be reaped from foreign investment is also shared by a majority of the public; all opinion polls carried out in 1990 point quite conclusively in that direction. In Poland, for instance, approval was found to range between 68 and 80 per cent. Although in every social group and most political parties there are people who take a critical view of foreign capital, their total number is small; paradoxically, there are more opponents on the far right than the left.

However, public opinion polls on the subject of foreign investment have been conducted in only some East European countries and their findings are not wholly credible (partly because of doubts about how representative the samples are). It seems probable that if such surveys had been made earlier – at the beginning of the decade, for instance – the degree of opposition to foreign investment would have been greater. After all, its perniciousness was for years a message drummed in by communist propaganda – though it now appears to have had little effect.

The fact that a significant majority of public opinion is in favour of foreign investment does not mean that every kind of activity by foreign enterprises is similarly approved. From the few polls containing more specific questions it has emerged that a large number of people are opposed to the sale of three types of property: land, print media, and natural wealth.

Land

The opponents are chiefly to be found among the rural population. It is significant that a large majority of them make no distinction between farmland and land with structures attached to it, so that some of the opponents of sales of land to foreigners have no objections to the sale of

buildings. Many foreign investors regard the purchase of the site of a
building as a matter of crucial importance since, although in theory in all
the countries of Eastern Europe they are allowed to rent land (and even take
out 'leases for life', i.e. for a term of ninety-nine years), such contracts are
viewed by foreign investors with considerable suspicion as a potential
source of disputes.

Media

A large percentage of persons polled are opposed to selling newspapers to
foreigners either on political grounds (it would give them too great an
influence on public opinion) or for moral reasons (for instance, there are
people who believe that foreign newspaper proprietors would peddle pornography) or both. Foreign investors have bought, at an exceptionally low
price for that matter, controlling interests in a large slice of the Hungarian
press. The governments of other East European countries are now anxious
to avoid committing the same mistake and are seeking to control privatization of the press (which, however, has not prevented some papers being
acquired by foreigners). Public opinion, on the other hand, seems to
entertain no great misgivings over the launching of new papers by foreign
proprietors.

Natural resources

Until recently the view that it was necessary to retain national sovereignty
over natural resources was the prevalent view. Cutbacks in mining production and even the closure of the most uneconomic mines have made a
large percentage of public opinion change its mind. At any rate, the conclusion in 1990 of the first contracts for exploitation of natural resources
(e.g. gas from coal deposits) met with no major protests.

Foreign investment is also opposed by some owners of small and the
least enterprising private establishments for fear that it might drive them
out of business.

These reservations apart (and for the most part they are not very significant), it can be said that the public in Eastern Europe attaches great hopes
to foreign investment. So we have a completely different situation from that
in many parts of Africa, Asia, and Latin America. The obvious question is,
why? The chief factor seems to be a general belief that foreign investment
can impart greater momentum to the process of modernization of societies
and move them 'closer to Europe'. The average citizen's knowledge of the
aims of foreign investors, the real dimensions of their operations, the
regulations governing them, and so on is very scant. It is a fair conclusion

that in practice the arrival of firms from the West is simply welcomed as heralding transplantation of one of the principal elements of a model that has worked for the richer nations.

East European governments must of course see foreign investment in far more complex terms than the popular view presented above, though for them, too, it is in effect also a prime consideration. But in their calculations it is the following positive effects of foreign investment that feature most prominently:

1 modernization – the transfer through foreign investment of ready-made technological and organizational models which will then permeate through to domestic enterprises;
2 growth of output – particularly welcome in the present situation of economic crisis;
3 balance-of-payments benefits;
4 increased market competition.

Conspicuous by its absence from this list is an item that features frequently in analyses of the benefits of foreign investment: increased employment. This is due to the fact that it is still very difficult to establish with any accuracy the probable net effect of such investment on employment. Obviously, construction of new factories by foreign enterprises creates new jobs; on the other hand, modernization of existing plants often results in lay-offs. East European governments have so far been unable to devise policies that would encourage investors to increase employment. However, a condition frequently laid down in the course of negotiations of sell-offs of state enterprises is that there will be no redundancies.

It should be added that East European governments are aware that foreign investment is a mixed blessing. Another point worth making is that in Eastern Europe, no less than in other parts of the world, one of the chief factors determining the present situation is the inertia of a bureaucratic machinery accustomed to the old ways of doing things and averse to change. Consequently there are considerable time-lags between the framing of policy by governments and its implementation, and foreign investors find themselves having to overcome all sorts of obstacles put in their way by officials, despite the wide support of governments, politicians, and the public. But this is a phenomenon that can also be observed in most other countries.

FOREIGN INVESTMENT AS A SPUR TO ECONOMIC MODERNIZATION

In practice expectations that foreign investment will speed up the modernization of East European economies are based on a number of premises. One of the most important is the hope that investors will in their own interests introduce modern organization and management methods in the factories owned or co-owned by them. That in effect means improving productivity – and the reserves in this area are very large. Labour productivity in East European industry is in most cases several times lower than in the EEC countries (though the differences are smaller in the northern part of the region in question and bigger in the south). Simplifying greatly, we can postulate that labour productivity is proportional to the size of gross national product per person employed. In 1986 this indicator in Yugoslavia was 14 per cent of the United States level, 20 per cent of the German, 23 per cent of the Italian, and 50 per cent of the Greek.[2] In Romania, Bulgaria, and Albania it was lower still.

The experience to date is that in virtually all cases the better organization introduced in factories belonging to foreign enterprises has led to a rapid and very marked increase in labour productivity which in turn ensures their owners higher rates of return.[3] This is so despite the fact that remuneration is usually much higher than in state enterprises (in view of payroll taxes and high social security contributions a large proportion of wages in foreign enterprises are paid in the form of various kinds of bonuses and fringe benefits).

Though any comparisons of productivity in different work-places are of course extremely debatable, the much better performance of foreign enterprises in this area is beyond question. Because of the inapplicability of other criteria, the Polish Chamber of Industry and Commerce used for the purpose of comparison the value of sales per person employed. It emerged that in 1989 in 949 foreign establishments, mostly small businesses, it was as much as 60 per cent higher than the average found in Poland's 500 biggest state enterprises.[4] In an earlier survey carried out in Yugoslavia in 1985 labour productivity in industry (defined as 'utilization of the means of production') was found to be 41 per cent higher in enterprises with a foreign capital stake than the national average.[5]

East European countries are banking on this situation recurring in the future. A typical example is the agreement (discussed in later chapters) for the takeover by Volkswagen of the Skoda enterprise in Czechoslovakia under which in 1997 employment will remain unchanged (22,000, including service departments), but that the number of cars produced will grow by 120 per cent (from 183,000 to 400,000 per annum) and their value even more pronouncedly.

It is not only shop-floor workers but also locally recruited management staff who are learning to work more efficiently, and these experiences are trickling down, albeit against considerable resistance, to indigenous enterprises. It is worth observing that for many of the employees hired by foreign enterprises the new routines and requirements they encounter (such as punctual clocking in and out, short breaks, rigorously enforced bans on drinking, etc.) come as a shock. For staff, no less startling is the system of management (e.g. lack of a multi-tier hierarchy pyramid) and many other innovations (e.g. discontinuance of the practice of maintaining huge stocks of raw materials on hand, typical of centrally controlled economies).

An important role in modernization of societies is also assigned to the transfer of modern technologies to Eastern Europe. Its countries' economies are technically backward, though the degree varies: many processes have an obsolescence of a few years, but many others of over twenty. In many lines of production (e.g. furniture) equipment is used which went out of date in the West fifty years ago. Installation of modern technologies by foreign investors is not easy and in former state factories often runs into resistance. A good example is the difficulty encountered in the introduction of microprocessors which automatically switch off the flow of electricity to idle machinery and so make it possible to measure the effective work-time of machinists; in state factories it was not only the shop floor but even management that balked at this. The introduction of such devices in foreign-owned factories is paving the way to their use in the rest of industry. Examples of this type are manifold.

Technology transfer is a very complex issue. Without a doubt, foreign investors will in their own interests implement it on a wide scale and in the most appropriate form: in their factories the introduction of new processes presents no major problems. Searching studies of technology transfer in Eastern Europe are very difficult undertakings, and the data used tend to come from less than fully objective questionnaires and reports submitted by foreign enterprises. The conclusion to be drawn from the incomplete statistics kept in a number of countries is that foreign investors invariably install much newer technologies than the ones in average use in national industry. In Yugoslavia 52 per cent of the foreign enterprises surveyed employed technologies five years old or less. In most instances they are the same technologies as those in the investor's parent company (in Yugoslavia this was the case in 84.6 per cent of enterprises).[6]

In the case of big multinationals it is, however, technologies still competitive on the world market but regarded as less attractive for the parent company that are the subject of transfer. This applies to many products. For instance, Renault opened an assembly plant in Yugoslavia for the R-4, production of which was shortly afterwards abandoned in France.

Foreign investment results, therefore, in transfers of technologies that are more modern than those hitherto used and reduces some of the development lag between the countries of destination and origin. It is, however, a palliative, not a long-run solution to the problem of technological advance.

Under present conditions a majority of enterprises cannot be expected to undertake costly research and development on a broad scale. In the case of enterprises owned by big international companies it is generally cheaper to transfer new processes from abroad than to develop them in Eastern Europe. Without a doubt, there will also be exceptions (for instance, the American company General Electric is engaging in a wide range of research in the Tungsram laboratories in Hungary), but not enough to relieve East European governments of R & D expenditures in key fields.

INCREASES IN PRODUCTION OF GOODS AND SERVICES

The improvements in productivity, transfer of high technology, and construction of new facilities brought by foreign investment usually lead to a growth of production and services. It is worth adding that the efficiency of foreign investment in Eastern Europe is as a rule much greater than that of indigenous projects. There are two reasons for this:

1 higher labour productivity;
2 better investment structure.

One of the characteristics of investment in Eastern Europe was the very high percentage of outlays on buildings and infrastructure in total capital formation. Expenditure on equipment was, therefore, relatively low, which of course reduced the efficiency of projects. Foreign enterprises make a point of carrying forward the least capital-intensive variety of investment, achieving a high rate of increase in production in relation to inputs. Given the small overall value of investment projects prior to 1990, the role of the foreign sector in the production of East European countries was of course comparatively modest; only in Yugoslavia, Hungary, and Poland did it account for 2 per cent of total output (2.5 per cent in Poland). The steep rise in foreign investment since 1990 has altered these proportions and resulted in foreign enterprises starting in 1991 to make their presence felt more strongly on the markets of these three countries. (In the others their share of output will remain small until 1992.)

The foregoing remarks apply only to total production. On an industry by industry basis the situation is of course highly differentiated. There are certain areas in which foreign enterprises, compared to their virtually negligible role in most branches of manufacturing and services (at any rate up to 1991), are by contrast conspicuously present. These include the hotel business, fruit processing, soft drinks, computers (production and maintenance), a wide range of building materials (e.g. tiles) and sports equipment. As foreign investment increases, so, too, does the number of products originating in foreign enterprises or joint ventures; in 1990, for instance, electric turbines and light bulbs and in 1991 pharmaceuticals and TV sets were added to the list. That, of course, is a general picture of the situation in Eastern Europe taken as a whole; there are considerable differences from country to country.

An increasingly important part in raising production is also being played by indirect investment. Often, though not always, even the purchase of a small portion (e.g. 10 per cent) of the equity of a previously wholly state-owned enterprise makes an appreciable difference to the size of output. Foreign investors usually manage in their own interests to improve capacity utilization rates. It is far from certain that this will continue to be the case in the future when the number of enterprises with foreign share-holders will be many times larger than at present.

Growth in output as a result of foreign investment is most easily attainable if the new owners embark on major capital expenditures. But it can also take place when these are very small (economists then refer to 'non-investment-led growth'). Theoretically, the potential for such growth of newly privatized state enterprises in Eastern Europe is immense. It has been estimated that in many factories the same hours of work and the same machinery could yield from 40 to 90 per cent more output given better organization, more intensive work, and so on. Significant increases in labour productivity are usually connected with not only more efficient organization but also higher rewards and certain additional investment outlays. The sum total of these additional financial inputs is, however, very small compared to the outputs obtained.

The majority of state factories work only a single shift; introduction of a second could double output. Theoretically, the combination of greater labour productivity and double day shifts could lead in a large number of factories to as much as a trebling of output without any major additional investment. In practice, it is usually found that the actual possibilities are much smaller for such reasons, among others, as scarcity of skilled personnel and the difficulties encountered in introducing new methods of organization. Changes will have to come about gradually and be spread over a number of years, and predictions of any kind in this field are extremely hazardous.

The growth in output obtained as a result of foreign investment is a particularly crucial factor in the situation of a recession. The segments of the economy in which there has been the heaviest commitment of foreign capital are ones in which increases in output have been substantial (with the exception of cosmetics and building materials) and contrast with other industries. Like all investment, foreign investment activates the multiplier principle in economic growth. However, this mechanism tends to operate in a different way than in the case of projects undertaken by indigenous enterprises in which a particularly large role is played by purchases of machinery and equipment. For technological reasons the plant installed by foreign enterprises usually has to be imported and purchases of additional equipment are very small. On the other hand, the nature and structure of foreign investment are such that production is made up to a very considerable extent of inputs by suppliers, which stimulates a growth of activity in other branches of the economy. This applies even to such enterprises as Tungsram in Hungary or Zamech in Poland which now farm out work to a larger number of indigenous subcontractors than before. That makes for expansion of the market for the latter's products and a specific modernization multiplier mechanism since the more exacting requirements of foreign enterprises compel suppliers to pay more attention to quality and precision, strict compliance with delivery schedules, and technological progress. It is worth adding that not all indigenous enterprises are capable of meeting these new challenges.

BALANCE-OF-PAYMENTS BENEFITS

The countries of Eastern Europe are banking on foreign investment helping to improve their balance of payments. There are three principal grounds for these expectations: export growth, import economies, and greater import-substitution. Part of the production of foreign enterprises and joint ventures with a foreign capital stake is earmarked for marketing abroad. It is easier for them to expand exports than for indigenous enterprises. Their output measures up more or less to the quality of Western goods, and an important role is also played by packaging, appearance, and compliance with world standards. Another advantage lies in these investors' foreign connections and, if they happen to be international corporations, possession of their own distribution and customer service networks in many parts of the world. The latter is a decisive factor in marketing such goods as automobiles, tractors, machine tools, furniture, or electrical household appliances.

Hopes of import savings spring from the fact that in the case of direct investment the bulk of the input usually takes the form of deliveries of machinery, equipment, and raw materials, the costs of which are, of course, met by the investor. Greater significance in the longer run may be assumed by the expansion of import-substitution production since foreign capital is very often drawn to industries in which domestic output is meager and antiquated and has, therefore, to be made up by imports on a considerable scale.

East European governments also had certain hopes of an influx of foreign capital in the form of cash. At the end of 1990, however, these hopes remained unrealized, the inward flow of money being infinitesimal.

In the case of projects undertaken by foreign enterprises on their own it is usually limited to financing the remuneration of the work-force in the period prior to the first production lines coming on stream (in some instances investors have been able to obtain credits from domestic banks and so spared even these expenditures). In joint ventures the bulk of disbursements in domestic currency is almost always met by the indigenous partner.

GROWTH OF MARKET COMPETITION

A further bonus of foreign investment is that it creates greater market competition. This is a crucial consideration in Eastern Europe. One of the characteristics of the planned economy model entrenched by over forty years of communist rule was a high degree of concentration in the output of a majority of staple products and a large proportion of others, supply being controlled by state trusts usually comprising no more than a handful of large enterprises. Very often this has resulted in a single firm having a complete monopoly in some commodity. This is the situation, for instance, with tractors in all the seven countries in question (except Czechoslovakia) and locomotives (everywhere except Albania where they are not manufactured). Where there are a number of producers there is a natural tendency to enter into informal arrangements. Indigenous small business is too weak to be a countervailing force. In these circumstances foreign enterprises can play a vital role in stimulating greater competition and are equipped for this purpose with major advantages (relatively high labour productivity, attractive design and packaging, and so on). Since the low degree of competitiveness is one of the main obstacles to the introduction of market mechanisms in Eastern Europe, expansion of foreign enterprise is a development to be particularly welcomed in this respect.

Growth of competitiveness is a major factor in forcing down production costs. This is now happening in, for instance, housing construction. In the past, a large majority of dwellings in Eastern Europe were built by large state enterprises which used uneconomic technologies and had extremely low productivity standards, but enjoyed a quasi-monopoly position on the market and a real one in the construction of medium and large buildings. Though the appearance of small, locally based private building contractors introduced certain elements of competition, these firms have tended to be poorly equipped technically and employ traditional technologies. The entry of a large number of foreign enterprises in Poland and Hungary has produced a breakthrough in this situation. It was suddenly discovered that housing could be built better, more cheaply, and, above all, faster. In a shrinking market hit by recession the example set by these foreign enterprises was bound to send ripples through the domestic construction business. A large number of bankruptcies have occurred (in the form of liquidation of enterprises). Some of the large state organizations have been hived off as private undertakings, and are now turning to more economic technologies. The foreign enterprises have not only survived but are continuing to expand, though many of them have had to restructure their operations – switching, for instance, to construction of single buildings rather than developments. The challenge from foreign enterprises has forced many indigenous firms to introduce a host of technological improvements – for instance, reduction of energy losses in buildings under construction.

Another example of the increased competition resulting from foreign investment is the situation on the toiletries market. As late as the mid-1980s Eastern Europe was, with the exception of Yugoslavia, still mainly producing items of the kind in use in the West in the 1930s. The entry of foreign enterprises resulted in the appearance of new products, previously available only as luxury imports, checked the bidding-up of prices, and forced indigenous enterprises to change their policy. We can conclude, therefore, that what East European governments are counting on is that inflows of foreign capital will be a source of revitalization in many sectors of industry, some of them being of great importance. Revitalization is seen as a factor facilitating dismantlement of the old system and construction of a free-market economy, speeding up economic modernization, and reducing production costs. The realization of these hopes will depend to a large extent on the scale of foreign investment.

SOME NEGATIVE CONSEQUENCES OF FOREIGN INVESTMENT

The benefits brought by foreign investment should not obscure the fact that there are also some less welcome facets. Easily overlooked in the early stages, they come as a total surprise even to those opponents who raise strident outcries over such essentially minor sticking-points as, for instance, the purchase of land by foreigners, but are blind to the real problems, familiar though these should be from what has long been observed in other parts of the world. Since every kind of economic activity, no matter how beneficial on balance, has its down side and so evokes popular criticism, a brief look at these negative consequences is necessary.

The governments of all countries which wish to attract foreign investment confront the same dilemma: if legislation is restrictive, foreign capital will stay away; if it is too liberal, profits will be removed abroad. Eastern Europe started by adopting highly restrictive regulations, erecting all sorts of barriers to the export of profits. With the passage of time it came to be seen that restrictions on transfers of profits had to be lifted if foreign investment was to be seriously encouraged. This view, which met with resistance in the higher echelons of the bureaucracy, prevailed in Poland and Hungary at the end of 1990, has won acceptance in Yugoslavia, and in 1991–2 will unquestionably also carry the day in the other countries of the region.

In the short run abolition of restrictions on export of profits creates no major problems as long as there are incentives to reinvest (tax reliefs for ploughed back retention, deductibility of expenditures on new capital assets). High profit rates will encourage most foreign enterprises to spend some of their earnings on new investment. Needless to say, some proportion of profits will inevitably be transferred; for one thing, there is the necessity of paying off the credits obtained by them from foreign banks to finance investment projects. But these sums are, and for the next year or so will remain, much smaller than the influx of new capital.

However, difficulties could well arise in the longer term since it is a reasonable assumption that profit rates will eventually start to flatten out. If the flow of new capital then begins to shrink, there would loom the painful problem of a profit drain from countries presently struggling as it is with acute debt service liabilities. This is a danger that is certain to materialize.

Problems of another kind are raised by the issue of government regulation of foreign enterprises. If attempts are made to subject them to state control, the flow of new funds will simply dry up; if no regulatory measures are taken, investors' behaviour will be guided solely by self-interest. In the affluent and well-organized countries of Western Europe it is relatively easy to induce foreign investors to act in accordance with national interests. One example is the use that has been made of foreign investment for regional development purposes by means of various tax reliefs, hidden subsidies, and so on. In Eastern Europe this is infinitely more difficult. In any case its new governments have not so far essayed anything in the way of a true regional policy. As a result foreign investment is concentrated in certain specified locations. In theory, these could in fact be underdeveloped regions with the lowest wage levels. In practice, foreign investors prefer to pay the somewhat higher wage costs of operating in the most developed and favourably situated areas, these being offset by a better infrastructure, all the advantages of the presence of other industries, and a relatively more efficient administration. The example of Yugoslavia also indicates that it is the most underdeveloped regions in which local tax contributions are heaviest, the authorities being solely concerned with immediate gains rather than long-term policy. The net effect could be to widen still further the economic disequilibria between different regions. It can, of course, be hoped that governments will eventually learn how to prevent this and devise policies aimed at persuading investors to take a greater interest in underdeveloped regions.

One of the greatest benefits of foreign investment is, as we have seen, that it stimulates a growth of labour productivity. This is both difficult and not without its negative side. Under communist rule there was a popular saying in all the East European countries that 'the government pretends to pay us and we pretend to work'. All the curses of this situation notwithstanding, there were certain blessings: the rhythm of work was very slow, frequent unscheduled rest pauses were probable, and rank-and-file employees were exposed to few stresses, being in little or no danger of dismissal. True, workers, particularly in the construction industry, tended to arrive at their work-places feeling the effects of exhausting commuting (car ownership is limited and public transport badly organized), but once there they could recover their strength (badly needed by many of them for the gruelling business of shopping after, or even during, work). The ease with which doctors handed out sick leave was a boon to family life – and also the widespread practice of 'moonlighting'. Now all this has changed. Though introduction of a market economy is easing the burdens of shopping, improving public transport, and so on, it is also ushering in new industrial relations. In the conditions obtaining in Eastern Europe rationalization of operations means having to work at a uniform, uninterrupted pace – and that is too much for a part of the work-force accustomed to different routines and practices. This is a source of stress and conflict.

In foreign enterprises earnings are (if we include all the fringe benefits) as a rule substantially higher than the national average, but so, too, are the requirements. Work-forces are not always willing or able to keep up with these, and one result is that the rises in labour productivity actually achieved are far smaller than the immense untapped potential.

A large proportion of the problems that are surfacing could be resolved by means of discussion and negotiation. Unfortunately, in most of the foreign enterprises in Eastern Europe there is no union organization: the owners are opposed, and employees are afraid of losing relatively well-paid jobs. This invited the introduction of 'military' styles of management. So far foreign investors have failed to realize that such a situation, though initially accepted, will sooner or later lead to industrial conflict.

Yet another kind of problem is created by the appearance on the East European market of factories owned by foreign investors which supply better and more attractive products. Though this has obvious spin-offs for the modernization of these economies, it also causes some difficulties. Let us take, for example, soft drinks production, an industry rated minor league, but with an output of considerable value and employing a far from small work-force. Until recently the market in most East European countries was dominated by various shoddy products made from recipes dating back to the 1930s, plus small quantities of drinks produced under licence (among them, Coca Cola and Pepsi Cola). Because the industry faced next to no competition it remained backward. In the last few years the East European market has been invaded by foreign enterprises offering better-quality and more attractively packaged drinks, partly made from imported concentrates. The suddenness of the appearance of this competition drove many domestic producers out of business (though most of them did not file bankruptcy petitions, but simply withdrew from the lucrative soft drinks market and set up in new lines). Employment in the industry fell, the most badly hit being small establishments in the provinces.

Similar developments occurred in, for example, cosmetics production and services. In the aggregate they are no bad thing from an economic point of view: better and more efficient producers drive out bad. The scale of this phenomenon is, for that matter, limited since foreign enterprises tend to go into areas of production in which there are shortages. Fears of such competition are nevertheless visible, particularly among the more conservative proprietors of private establishments, and will grow greater, but so, too, will the interest of firms in Eastern Europe in entering into partnership with foreign enterprises.

Fears of foreign investment are also kindled by certain mistakes that have been committed through lack of experience. These include the sale at an unbelievably low price of a large part of the Hungarian press to foreign publishing concerns or the leasing – also for a song – of the technically best-equipped department of the Gdansk Shipyard to a person with no capital or ties with foreign shipbuilders. Fortunately, such blunders have been relatively rare.

Summing up, we can say that very great hopes are placed by East European governments and societies in foreign investment. It is likely that these expectations will be largely fulfilled. But for that, these nations will have to pay a certain price and, above all, learn how to work more efficiently. Changes in the pace of work, increased competition on the national market, and transfers of profits abroad will all go a little against the grain, but on balance East Europeans can be expected to continue to regard foreign enterprise with favour.

3 Evolution of legal regulations and their impact on foreign investment

GENERAL REMARKS

The positive attitude of host governments and the public does not decide the realization of foreign investments. If projects are actually to be undertaken a whole series of other conditions also have to be fulfilled. Among the most crucial are adequate laws and other rules relating to investment and taxation. Theorists often believe that regulations issued on important matters reflect the current policy of the government and dominant political forces of a given country. In practice, however, this is not the case. There is always a time-lag between changes in government policy and changes in legislation. In Eastern Europe the gap may be a long one, especially as there are objective conditions standing in the way of change.

In each country there are thousands of regulations that need to be amended. The public administration is inefficient, and even civil servants in very senior positions are often ill-prepared. For example, from my conversations with Bulgarian and Czechoslovak officials in 1989 and 1990 I came away with the impression that, however well qualified in many departments, many of them had no grasp of such things as the difference between a share and a bond, let alone how stock exchanges actually work. Judging by the numerous articles in the national press of Eastern Europe, the situation in other countries was (at any rate up to the end of 1990) no better. Small wonder then that a large proportion of the legislative material prepared in government departments was badly drafted and contained basic flaws and inconsistencies. These bills then went to parliament where they were corrected by conscientious but not necessarily knowledgeable deputies. As a result many of the new laws, including those relating to foreign investment, have been rightly criticized as piecemeal and internally contradictory. Governments have responded to such criticism by having the bills in question redrafted, which usually produces a new version that is both a little more coherent and more favourable to foreign investors. If we compare the regulations of the 1970s and the rules now in force we will see a very marked change for the better. The shape of laws and regulations is, therefore, being steadily improved, a fact that is registering increasingly favourably with foreign firms.

The fact that changes in the rules governing the operation of foreign enterprises proceed in the right direction for business is one thing; the frequency with which they are being made is another. The funds committed by investors are usually not their own, but borrowed. To obtain a bank loan they have to submit a whole raft of documents, including an evaluation of the profitability of a project. Needless to say, frequent changes in regulations make any kind of realistic appraisal impossible and so complicate the obtaining of credits. In many cases banks simply refuse to provide any backing at all.

If the overall direction of changes in regulations offers a better deal for foreign investors it does not by any means follow that this can be said of all of them. Far from it: in some cases they actually worsen the situation. This, of course, is not popular and does not encourage a growth of investment. Evidently, East European governments have not yet grasped the crucial importance of stable rules. In practice, the desired result could be achieved in one of two ways:

1 by strict adherence to the principle that amendments in regulations cannot worsen the conditions under which foreign enterprises operate (in other words, any changes in rules can only apply to future investment projects);
2 by drawing up and giving statutory force to comprehensive Investment Codes (generally regarded as legal acts of superior force, codes are rarely changed in Eastern Europe).

In theory, the stability of rules has been guaranteed in one East European country: Yugoslavia. In practice, however, even in Yugoslavia there is one basic area in which this does not apply: the taxation system which is subject to continual amendment by the local, republican, or federal authorities.

However undesirable frequent changes in regulations may be, the laws currently in force cannot be seen as adequate. They have to be amended, and this is indeed the intention of the governments concerned.

YUGOSLAVIA

The first East European country in which foreign investment could be undertaken under a general system of binding rules was Yugoslavia. It was apparent from the start that its leaders were steering an unsteady course between trying to revitalize the economy and preserving the 'socialist purity' of their country's system. Needless to say, these waverings were also reflected in legislation. The first regulations permitting foreign investment were issued as early as 1967. In the next twenty-one years (to 1988) there came a host of further regulatory measures which differed considerably from one another but had one feature in common: they denied foreign investors full ownership of factors of production. Foreign investors granted the right to participation in management and profit taking, but not to ownership. The only form of activity allowed foreign enterprises were 'contractual joint ventures' in which the relationship between the parties was, as the name indicates, purely contractual. The foreign investment did not change the character of the enterprise in which it was made; it remained a public sector enterprise and did not become a true joint venture company.[1]

Under the Yugoslav constitution only the self-management council can be the owner of an enterprise. Recognition of investors' right to profits does not mean that they can remit them at will. That being so, it is no surprise that foreign investment in Yugoslavia was small: in 1968–88 only 380 joint ventures were set up and the total amount of capital invested is placed at 340 million dollars.[2] A large proportion of these projects were undertaken by foreign enterprises which aimed at getting their money back not so much in the form of profits as of highly paying exports (payments in foreign currencies for imports were authorized). A case in point is Renault which financed the construction of a car-kit plant in Nove Mesto near Ljubljana to which the components are shipped from France.

It is symptomatic that even the far from liberal regulations previously in force in Yugoslavia were attacked by conservative communists who saw the very presence of foreign enterprises as a threat. The tug of war between the party's hard-liners and reformers had a direct effect on the course of foreign investment legislation in the period in question. The 1967 regulations allowed foreigners no more than a 49 per cent stake in joint ventures (in other words, the controlling interest was mandatorily held by the Yugoslav partner) and the duration of the company had to have a specified time-limit. In 1973 a series of laws relating to foreign investment, licences, co-production, etc. were passed which to some extent liberalized the 1967 legislation. The trend went into reverse in 1978 when a new package of legislation regulating external economic cooperation was approved. One of the most fiercely criticized clauses stipulated that the rate of return on capital employed by foreign investors could not exceed 'the level of average profitability of the sector within which the respective joint venture operated'.[3] In effect Yugoslav bureaucrats were given a free hand in determining the size of foreign enterprises' profits. Liberal communists succeeded in getting this restriction lifted in 1984 when new and less stringent regulations were introduced. However, they still left unresolved the problem of ownership, which for potential investors is the heart of the matter.

A fundamental change did not come until 1988. By then Yugoslavia had slid into hyperinflation and the deteriorating economic situation was compounded by mounting political dissensions. The Yugoslav government came to the conclusion that no stone could be left unturned in efforts to put the economy back on its feet. A gradual jettisoning of ideological dogmas was decided upon. One of the most important steps was the introduction of amendments in the constitution which in effect spelled 'the beginning of the end' of the self-management system. The 1988 regulations finally gave foreign investors in Yugoslavia the right to own enterprises and acquire equity in joint ventures. Since then virtually all types of investment are open to foreign capital: contractual joint ventures, equity joint ventures, and wholly foreign-owned companies. Foreign investors may now buy out domestic partners' shares of a joint venture or purchase a domestic private company or public sector enterprise. There are no longer any restrictions on possession of real estate. Ownership of mining concessions is also permitted.[4] The Yugoslav constitution guarantees the basic rights of foreign investors, including a share of profits proportional to their investment and transfer of profits to other countries. More important still, it stipulates that only the laws in force at the time that an investment agreement is signed are applicable; new and less favourable regulations cannot later be imposed.

Yugoslavia, therefore, now has very liberal foreign investment rules. In many areas – including the fundamental question of profit remittances – it is over two years ahead of the rest of Eastern Europe. Also of crucial importance are the constitutional guarantees given to foreign investors. However, there are certain gaps. One of these is taxation, and the tax regime in Yugoslavia is infinitely complex because of the differences in the rates at which it is levied by each republic and local authority. For instance, at the end of 1990 tax on the profits of equity joint ventures came to only 0.9 per cent in Kosovo, compared to 8 per cent in Macedonia, Serbia, and Voivodina (and, in this last republic, even 12 per cent on some activities).[5] In the case of contractual investments the rate is 10 per cent, but there is an exemption for foreign nationals if they reinvest profits or deposit them in a Yugoslav bank.

One of the most troublesome problems for foreign investors in Yugoslavia in the so-called 'contributions' which are in effect additional taxes levied by republican and local authorities to provide finance for public services and utilities. They include assessments at a high level on gross wages and salaries, the rate ranging from 27 per cent in Serbia to as much as 60 per cent in Macedonia, and on incomes, the rate ranging from approximately 8 per cent in Macedonia and Montenegro to 30 per cent in

Serbia. Investors, initially attracted by liberal legislation, are often subsequently put off by the practices of local authorities and the tax system. A large proportion – some 39 per cent – of foreign investment was directed towards small Slovenia whose public administration is generally thought to be the best organized. This offsets the much higher wage levels than in other republics.

It is worth adding that there are also certain other restrictions imposed on foreign investors. For example, wholly foreign-owned companies are barred from telecommunications, air transport, publishing, and broadcasting. All enterprises with a foreign capital stake are subject to strict labour relations laws. Employees may be dismissed for breaches of discipline specified in the company's by-laws; the disputes that arise in such cases often lead to prolonged litigation. Employees may also be dismissed if their jobs are made redundant for technological or other reasons, but in such cases the employer must guarantee them employment in another company, early retirement with full pension rights, or compensation of at least two years' average earnings.

The federal and some of the republican governments are thinking of relaxing many of the existing restrictions (in the field of labour relations, for instance) and introducing a more rational tax system. It was realised in independent Slovenia, where the government hopes that the influx of foreign investment will help to restructure the economy.

POLAND

In Poland the door to foreign direct investment was first opened by a government decree of 14 May 1976 which permitted the establishment of small businesses by foreign nationals of Polish extraction. Under these regulations firms could now be wholly owned by citizens of other countries. They were to operate on the basis of licences issued by local authorities (in practice strictly controlled by central government) which specified precisely what and how much they were allowed to produce. Public officials kept a close watch on compliance with these obligations and there were cases of foreign firms being penalized for making goods for which there was market demand but were not itemized in their concessions. Despite all the bureaucratic obstacles, the number of these so-called 'Polonia' firms grew rapidly, though from the outset the owners included persons whose Polish ancestry (a requirement in any case often hard to establish) was purely fictitious.

In the 1980s the rules governing foreign enterprises were subject in Poland to the sort of frequent changes observed in other East European countries. On the one hand, there was a gradual expansion of the scope of foreign investment, while on the other, often unfavourable modifications to the tax system.

The 1976 decree contained many clauses which were inconsistent with earlier regulations but which were not rescinded. The best solution to such contradictions could only be an overriding enactment by the supreme legislative branch of government. The Polish extraction requirement, ignored in practice, also needed to be scrapped. This was accomplished in 1982 with the adoption by parliament of a law 'On Business Activity in Small Industry Conducted by Foreign Legal and Natural Persons'. The result of this liberal measure was an abrupt rise in the number of foreign small businesses registered. (In 1982 and 1983 no less than 415 such enterprises were licenced).

The growth of the foreign ownership sector was thought too rapid by some communists, and the liberal provisions of the new law viewed with dismay by officials responsible for overseeing foreign investment. The upshot was that only a year later, in 1983, the basic aims of the 1982 Act were stultified by new regulations which, among other things, raised the rate of corporation income tax from 50 to 80 per cent. So hefty a tax seemed likely to put foreign firms out of business. In actual fact most of them managed to survive.

Theoretically, the 1982 Act provided for the establishment of small businesses. However, Polish legislation has never laid down a definition of this term and, although its absence enabled some firms to expand considerably in a short period of time, by and large its effect was to deter the large foreign investors. The division of foreign enterprises into large and small is artificial and drawing a line presents awkward practical problems. Government advisers recommended drafting a new law which would give foreign enterprises greater freedom of action, a better tax deal, and guarantees of exemption from any changes in regulations unfavourable to them. Officials responsible for foreign investment did not accept this point of view and drew up a bill which applied only to large enterprises. They obtained certain tax preferences (a reduction in corporation income tax to 50 per cent with allowances for exports or reinvestment). Unfortunately, they were simultaneously required to enter into partnerships with Polish enterprises (though they could apply for this rule to be waived) and received no effective insurance against nationalization. The director-general and president of the company's governing board had to be Polish citizens. This bill was passed by parliament on 23 April 1985. It was criticized from the outset and it soon became evident that it would have to be superseded.

The next law – 'On Economic Activity with the Participation of Foreign Parties' – was enacted on 23 December 1988 and amended on 28 December

1989.[6] It greatly increased the opportunities for foreign investors, offering them four possibilities:

1 a limited liability or joint stock company with 100 per cent of the equity held by them;
2 a limited liability or joint stock company with the equity shared with Polish or foreign partners;
3 a joint stock company (with foreign or Polish partners) with capital raised through public subscription;
4 acquisition of shares in Polish limited liability or joint stock companies.[7]

Polish partners can be chosen entirely at will. Limited liability or joint companies are formed under the rules of the still-binding 1934 Commercial Code. There is no limitation on the size of the operation.

The new regulations have been welcomed by foreign investors, but with one, though very important, exception: the provisions relating to repatriation of profits. Since 1 January 1990 foreign enterprises can remit 15 per cent of the profits from sales in Poland (a percentage that is expected to be increased in due course) and also any balance of export earnings over import expenditures. The taxes payable are relatively low compared to domestic enterprises. Corporation income tax is 40 per cent of assessed earnings and there is a three-year exemption period.[8] Foreign enterprises also pay a turnover tax (at a rate of 20 per cent in production and 5 per cent on sales of goods and services) and payroll, real estate, and local taxes.[9] An innovation welcomed by investors is a provision that if any changes are made in corporation income tax enterprises already registered will pay it at the old rate until the end of 1995.

Foreign enterprises which wish to purchase land have to obtain permission from the Minister of Internal Affairs. But such approval is not necessary for leasing (and in the case of state-owned land there is a possibility of perpetual leases).

The formalities required of foreign investors setting up enterprises have been considerably simplified and they can call on the assistance of the Foreign Investment Agency. A statutory period has been set for the consideration of applications, but it is relatively long, amounting to two months.[10]

The 1988 law regulates the operation of medium and large foreign enterprises and joint ventures. The majority of small businesses are still bound by the 1982 law and its 1989 amendments (which included tax reductions).

The legislation as it stood, was widely criticized not only by foreign investors but also by Polish officials. Since the beginning of 1990 there has been general agreement, shared by the Foreign Investment Agency and the Ministry of Foreign Economic Relations, that the rules need to be changed. Sterile discussions continued over the shape of the new regulations, months went by, and the rules remained unchanged for more than a year. Some badly prepared projects of new regulations were rejected. Finally, on 7 July 1991, a new bill was adopted. It introduces some very significant changes in the foreign investment rules. The most important provision is the waiving of all restrictions on remittance of profits, dividends, and capital gains.

The law of 1991 states that foreign enterprises are no longer required to obtain the approval of the state administration, except in some activities like the administration of ports and airports, manufacture of armaments, creation of consulting enterprises and trade in real estate. The Foreign Investment Agency, issuing permissions until 1991, is now transformed into an information office. Enterprises and investing more than 2 million ECU (about 2.6 million dollars) are getting three-year tax holidays. Longer tax holidays are given to foreign enterprises investing in specified regions, in export-oriented activities and to factories introducing modern techniques. The Polish government has thus satisfied the principal requirements of potential investors.

HUNGARY

The first regulations permitting direct foreign investment in Hungary were issued in 1972. In the next fifteen years they were frequently revised, though the amendments were, apart from a cut in taxes, relatively minor. The situation in 1987 was that foreign nationals and companies could operate in Hungary only as partners in joint ventures with domestic enterprises. Their equity holding could not exceed 40 per cent, though in special cases permission might be obtained for a larger share. Remittances of hard currency could only be made out of export earnings. Corporate income tax was levied at a rate of forty per cent and there were a large number of investment incentives (including a five-year tax holiday for projects in priority sectors of the economy). In contrast to most other East European countries at this time, no posts in such joint ventures were specifically reserved for Hungarian citizens.

Hungarian governments did a good public relations job of promoting the foreign investment opportunities in their country. Throughout the 1980s Western businessmen thronged to Budapest in their thousands, many enjoying the fare at the city's restaurants. However, on closer acquaintance with the regulations and conditions, few of them actually decided to invest. It then became obvious that the regulations had to be modified.

The necessary changes were introduced in 1988–90. In 1988 there came Law XXIV on Foreign Investments which simplified the formalities involved in setting up joint ventures and made repatriation of profits easier (though still restricting it to enterprises' hard currency earnings). The interpretation of the rules, especially in the case of tax reliefs, was a source of prolonged debate, which caused many potential investors to hold back. In the end new regulations came into effect in July 1990 which denied reliefs to enterprises in which the foreign capital stake is less than 20 per cent (or 5 million forints), though this provision has been attacked by critics including the Minister of Industry and Trade.[11]

The next change in the rules was made on 1 January 1991. Tax reliefs are now granted only to firms involved in certain particularly important sectors of the economy and only if the foreign equity holding exceeds 30 per cent and the nominal capital 50 million forints. At the same time the launching of foreign enterprises no longer requires the approval of any government office; all that is needed are a certified agreement and court registration.

Foreigners can own 100 per cent of the equity of enterprises. They can perform the functions of enterprise directors. Foreign investors' earnings can be repatriated without limitation. In the case of nationalization, the Hungarian government guarantees the indemnity in hard currency, estimated at the enterprise's market value. This last point is considered to be particularly important to many small investors.

THE CZECH AND SLOVAK FEDERAL REPUBLIC

The legal status of foreign enterprises in Czechoslovakia has been even more strongly affected by political factors than elsewhere. Up to the Second World War it was a country with an exceptionally heavy foreign capital involvement. After the outbreak of war the majority of enterprises were transferred to German ownership, which facilitated the post-war process of nationalization. In the 1950s foreign investment in Czechoslovakia was out of the question. Subsequently a number of agreements were concluded which allowed foreign enterprises to undertake a handful of projects (mostly hotel construction), but without ownership rights.

From 1969 to 1989 Czechoslovakia was ruled by the communists put in power as a direct result of the Soviet intervention in 1968. They were more concerned with preserving 'ideological purity' than the rest of Eastern Europe and for a long time emphatically rejected the idea of attracting foreign direct investment and continued to stand firm even after most other governments had started swinging round to such a policy. The door to foreign investment was not opened until 1986 when regulations were issued permitting the establishment of joint ventures. However, the foreign capital stake could not exceed 49 per cent and a majority holding had to be retained by a Czechoslovak enterprise (or enterprises). The operations of these joint ventures were confined to industrial production. The question of profit transfers was regulated by means of permits decided on a case-by-case basis. Foreign investors received no guarantees that the provisions for remittances, taxation, etc. would not be subject to change at some future date. Income tax was set at 50 per cent and there were no additional tax incentives. A levy of 25 per cent was imposed on hard currency remittances. One of the most restrictive clauses was that key management positions had to be filled by Czechoslovak citizens. The net effect of these rules was that foreign investment in Czechoslovakia remained next to negligible until the end of 1989.

Following the assumption of power by non-communists in December 1989, the government issued a string of declarations proclaiming its interest in attracting foreign investment, and a large number of Western businessmen paid visits to Czechoslovakia. However, behind the scenes a struggle was being waged between advocates of full-blooded reform (whose most prominent spokesman is Finance Minister Vaclav Klaus) and supporters of a slower, more gradual approach (who include the former Deputy Prime Minister Valter Komarek). The first succeeded in 1990 in pushing through a series of laws which facilitated foreign investment; meanwhile the second faction is tending to slow down their practical implementation (for instance, through a lack of the appropriate schedules).

As a result of the haste with which the new legislation was cobbled together, and possibly deliberate action by senior officials, some of it is badly drafted, incomplete, and even internally contradictory. This last criticism applies, for instance, to the crucial question of land ownership: one of the new laws forbids foreign investors to purchase land, but at the same time allows them to form enterprises, wholly owned by them, which can buy land. Many regulations are treated as temporary stopgaps which will be changed following the adoption of a new Commercial Code in 1991.

The key role for foreign investors is now played by a 'Law on Enterprises with Foreign Property Participation', commonly called 'the joint venture law', passed on 1 May 1990. Under its provisions foreign investors can form wholly owned subsidiaries established and governed by Czechoslovak law (these subsidiaries are, confusingly, called joint venture companies). Through these companies, foreign investors may buy land or existing Czechoslovak companies. They can also start 'normal' joint venture companies, either with individuals or with corporate entities. The procedure for issuing licences to foreign enterprises has been simplified and is supervised by an Agency for Foreign Investment set up in July 1990.

Corporation income tax has been reduced to 40 per cent, but the tax on dividends remains at 25 per cent.[12] On 1 January 1991 the krone became internally convertible, but foreign enterprises are still required to sell all their hard currency revenues to the state, though they are entitled to buy back 70 per cent of them for the purpose of repatriating profits or paying for imported goods.

Foreign investment is overseen by the Ministry of Finance. With a view to speeding up the process, since 1990 it is required to process applications by prospective foreign enterprises within sixty days. Another 1990 decision provides for the joint venture law to be amended by the end of 1992.

ROMANIA

Incredible as it may seem today, Romania was the second East European country to permit foreign investment. The first regulations to that effect were issued in 1971 and supplemented by Decree No.424 in 1972. They allowed foreign investors to enter into partnerships with Romanian enterprises (*de facto* state-owned), but with no more than a 49 per cent holding. Transfers of profits could only be made out of the joint venture's hard currency earnings, usually obtained from exports. Conditions in Romania, bureaucratic inefficiency and corruption not least among them, effectively discouraged investors and the flow of foreign capital was very small. Little difference was made by an improvement in the tax system; at the end of 1987 income tax amounted to only 30 per cent and the tax on profit remittances to 10 per cent. New joint ventures were made exempt from taxation for their first year and entitled to tax reliefs for the next two.[13]

More significant changes came with Decree-Law No.96 of 14 March 1990 which permitted foreign investment in virtually all sectors of the economy (including agriculture, banking, insurance, industry). Foreign investors can now be not only partners in joint ventures but also the sole owners of enterprises. A certain problem is created by the requirement of very detailed articles of incorporation, observance of which is overseen by the public administration. Foreign enterprises may be directly involved in export operations.

Potential investors were unhappy with the profit-transfer regulations. All export earnings had to be deposited with the Romanian Foreign Trade Bank or other authorized institutions from which they were not always easily withdrawable. Theoretically, foreign investors were also entitled to remit 8 per cent of their net profits in the domestic currency (leu). Corporation income tax remained very low, the rate still amounting to only 30 per cent as before, and for the first two years there is an exemption.

On 29 March 1991, a Foreign Investment Law was passed which makes certain amendments to the previous regulations. Some restrictions have been lifted and the registration of foreign firms was made easier (it is now automatic if the Romanian Development Agency does not object within thirty days from the date of the application). In the event of nationalization investors are guaranteed compensation to the level of the real value of their holdings. Investors are exempt from payment of the tax on profits from investment in industry, agriculture, and the construction sector for a period of five years, and in other sectors of the economy for a period of two or three years. Substantial additional tax reliefs are offered to enterprises which reinvest their profits in Romania. Most of the other regulations have remained unchanged.[14]

BULGARIA

The first post-war regulations permitting foreign investment were issued in 1980. They were very liberal. Together with subsequent additions and amendments (1981–7) they allowed the creation of foreign enterprises of unlimited duration and in all sectors of the economy. Taxation was very low, amounting to 10 per cent on profits transferred abroad and 20 per cent on income. In the latter case there was also the possibility of a three-year tax holiday. Remittances could only be made out of export earnings. Engagement of non-Bulgarian nationals as president and managing director was forbidden. Another hurdle was the necessity of obtaining a licence from the Council of Ministers for creating a partly or wholly foreign-owned enterprise. Numerous additional regulations required various other licences and made foreign enterprises subject to irksome bureaucratic oversight.

On 13 January 1989 Decree No.56 'On Economic Activity' was issued. Articles 99 to 126 deal with foreign direct investment. The formalities connected with setting up joint ventures have been simplified if the foreign capital stake is less than 49per cent, and 20 per cent in the case of joint stock companies. Income tax is levied at a rate of 15 per cent. Profits of foreign partners can be transferred abroad without restriction.

Foreign enterprises are theoretically entitled to own real property, but only on a time-limited basis. The Decree rules that 'when the foreign party ceases its activity in Bulgaria the local party or the State acquire its property rights. Foreign firms may not have any ownership rights in immovable properties such as land and forests and in natural resources.'

ALBANIA

Until 1990 foreign direct investment in Albania was impossible. All forms of foreign ownership were specifically banned by the constitution. In the second half of 1990, as a result of political changes, the Albanian rulers relaxed some of their ideological rigidity and decided to follow the example of other East European countries and open the door to foreign investment. The constitution was amended to that effect and new regulations on foreign enterprise were issued. Foreigners may now own up to 90 per cent of the equity of enterprises started in Albania. The only forms investment can take are joint ventures in which one of the partners must be an Albanian state enterprise. Earnings may be remitted after payment of tax. Special incentives have been promised to investors, particularly in the fields of food processing, textile manufacturing and tourism.[15]

Changing regulations have, needless to say, had a basic effect on the volume of foreign direct investment in Eastern Europe. Prior to the 1970s it was non-existent if we exclude the complicated operations discussed above, such as the Yugoslav 'contractual joint ventures', which yielded profits but gave the investor no property rights.

A second stage was ushered in with the sanctioning of investment as a minority partner of indigenous enterprises in joint ventures controlled by the state. The sole exception to this rule was the 'Polonia' small business scheme in Poland (exceptions were also made in some of the other countries, but of an *ad hoc* nature). It was not till the 1980s that enterprises wholly owned by a foreign investor were allowed into Eastern Europe. It is significant that in many official translations of legal texts (and not infrequently even in the original wording) all foreign enterprises are called 'joint ventures' even if they have only one owner. There are many more such examples of confusion of terms, one of the most curious being 'one-person companies' (which include 'state one-person companies').

The process of changing the rules governing the operation of foreign enterprises in Europe will continue. In due course other countries can be expected to adopt the principles developed in Poland, Hungary, and Yugoslavia. Everything indicates that by 1995 at the latest the whole region will have introduced regulations similar to those in force in the EEC countries, with tax systems much more favourable than in Western Europe.

4 Reasons for investing in Eastern Europe

The volume of foreign investment in Eastern Europe and the number of new enterprises created as a result have been snowballing for a number of years. In 1986 there were barely a thousand such enterprises, of which 650 were small businesses set up in Poland. At the end of 1989 this total had climbed to just under 3,000 and at the end of 1990 to over 7,000. The volume of capital invested has grown even faster: from less than 300 million dollars in 1986 to over 2 billion in 1990. The approved investment programmes of foreign enterprises had at the turn of 1991 passed the 4.5 billion dollar mark.

It is very difficult to list in order of importance the true motives for Western investors' involvement in Eastern Europe, especially as the situation keeps changing. For small and medium firms the fundamental consideration in most cases is the direct returns on capital; but for large companies increasing weight is attached to certain other factors, such as enhancing the position of the company, the possibilities of economies of scale, exploitation of technological advantages, securing an assured market, etc.

An important role is often also played by a circumstance of a more specific nature: ethnic ties. Among the millions of emigrants (or their descendants) from Eastern Europe now living in North America and Western Europe there are some who have amassed considerable fortunes and are prepared to invest some of their funds in the 'old country'. Because of the significance of this factor in the present initial phase of foreign investment I will give it pride of place here.

THE ETHNIC FACTOR

The number of people of East European extraction living in the West is hard to establish with any precision: various estimates place them at between 15 and 21 million (of which from 10 to 14 million are Polish). Even the lower of these figures indicates the potential role of these East European ethnic groups. The vast majority (95 per cent) of the original immigrants were peasants and unskilled workers, and most of them started out in menial employment. By the second and third generation most of their descendants had attained earnings brackets somewhat above the mean level in their countries and in the case of the largest group (Polish Americans) average income was over 110 per cent of that for the whole population. Nevertheless, until the end of the 1970s the number of businesses owned by East European ethnics was still on the small side.

In the 1980s the situation changed appreciably. Over 1.5 million people emigrated from Eastern Europe and a large proportion of them were energetic and well-trained professionals. It was not long before many of this new wave of immigrants began starting their own businesses or filling executive posts in other companies. Thus the opening of Eastern Europe to foreign investment at the end of the 1980s coincided with the emergence of sizeable and relatively affluent expatriate communities. A combination of emotional ties and the more mundane wish to put their funds to profitable use and expand their own usually smallish firms inclined a considerable number of East European immigrants to look for investment opportunities in their old countries.

This phenomenon was first observed in Yugoslavia whose situation is a special one. It was for a long time the only East European country in which travel to the West was relatively free and which permitted economic migration (regulated by agreements with a number of West European countries). Some of these emigrants became naturalized citizens of the countries to which they had moved, but nevertheless continued to remit considerable sums for investment in Yugoslavia – in, for instance, the construction of houses, cafes, restaurants, garages, etc., many of them registered in the names of relatives still living there. These streams of small individual remittances added up to a large aggregate inflow of capital but technically fell short of creating a foreign ownership sector. Such expatriate investment contributed to the development of a great belt of territory along the Adriatic coast and also of many inland regions (including parts of the once very depressed areas of Bosnia).

The regulations effectively prevented investment by expatriates in productive facilities. This was partly changed by the 1988 Foreign Investments Act under which:

> Yugoslavs who have permanent residence outside the territory of this country can obtain the status of foreign investors [regardless of citizenship]. Such Yugoslav nationals are considered foreign investors as long

as they do not take up residence in Yugoslavia. . . . However, if they return to Yugoslavia they forfeit the privileges enjoyed by foreign investors.[1]

In practice this forces returned owners of enterprises to make regular visits abroad (to neighbouring Italy or Austria, for instance) for periods just long enough to be technically classified as non-resident in Yugoslavia. Despite these legal intricacies, the influx of capital belonging to Yugoslav emigrants grew considerably in 1990.

The second country to set its sights on utilization of the funds of its ethnics was Poland where, as mentioned earlier, regulations permitting the creation of so-called 'Polonia' enterprises were issued in 1976. At first the response was small as can be seen from the number of licences issued (in a few cases the persons or firms obtaining them did not in fact start businesses): six in 1977, eight in 1978, twelve in 1979, thirty five in 1980, and fifty two in 1981. At the turn of 1982 the number of 'Polonia' enterprises actually operating in Poland totalled roughly a hundred, of which about sixty belonged to persons of Polish extraction, a dozen or so to persons with Polish spouses, and about twenty-five to foreign nationals with no Polish blood or other ties whatsoever. The much more liberal law passed in 1982 created an almost overnight boom of interest in investment resulting in 1982 and 1983 in a steep rise in the number of foreign-owned enterprises registered in Poland: by 235 in 1982 and 180 in 1983.[2] Slightly over half of these new businesses belonged to persons of Polish extraction and the owners of most of the others had some kind of Polish affiliation (birth, extraction, or marriage).

These enterprises were involved in a wide variety of fields, mainly in industry and the production of such goods as building materials, foodstuffs, clothing, lingerie, timber products, synthetics, cosmetics, metalware, furs, leather wear, electronic equipment, and medical supplies, but a large number were also set up in the services sector. In the latter area there was also considerable interest in investment in small hotels and pensions, but here bureaucratic barriers proved particularly formidable and no significant numbers of facilities of this kind were opened by foreign nationals.

The activity of these usually small but dynamic enterprises was from the outset vehemently criticized not only by communist hard-liners, but also by many managers of large factories in the public sector and senior bureaucrats. For one thing, they tended to cream off the best personnel employed by state industry, which could not be expected to arouse much enthusiasm; for another their high level of profits aroused both jealousy and alarm (confirming belief in the inefficiency of public enterprise). At the end of 1983 the Polish government decided, largely no doubt on ideological grounds, to alter some of the rules governing foreign-owned enterprises. The most crucial change was an increase in income tax to 80 per cent (with minor allowances for export production). The effect was an abrupt drop in the number of new businesses started in the small-scale industry sector and the closing of a large number of others (see Table 4.1).

Table 4.1 Foreign small businesses registered in Poland

Year	1981	1982	*1983*	*1984*	*1985*	*1986*	*1987*	*1988*
Number started	52	235	180	138	71	18	51	67
Number wound up	5	5	12	22	32	42	27	25

Source: J. Kwiatkowski, 'Zagraniczne inwestycje bezposrednie w krajach Europy Wschodniej', *Sprawy Miedzynarodowe*, 1990, No.1. pp. 88, 89.

In 1988 and 1989 there followed another series of changes in regulations which reduced the rate of income tax and relaxed some of the restrictions on small business. These produced a second upswing in the number of new enterprises, most of them started, as in the past, by persons of Polish extraction. Some of these firms were registered under the regulations relating to joint ventures.

Foreign-owned small businesses involved in manufacturing vary greatly in size. A substantial majority are indeed small (over 90 per cent employ less than 100 persons), but as early as 1986 there were four with payrolls of over 500. Total employment in these enterprises rose quickly: from a mere 12,200 in 1982 to no less than 53,400 in 1985 and 71,000 in 1988. Even faster was the rate at which their sales and exports grew. A further point worth noting is that almost all the businesses started under the 1982 law which employed over 100 persons belonged to proprietors of Polish extraction.

Following the formation of the first non-communist government in Eastern Europe, Poland began to attract the interest not only of small entrepreneurs contemplating expansion of their spheres of activity, but also of members of ethnic Polish communities with much more substantial funds at their disposal. They entered into negotiations with a view to acquiring numerous large industrial establishments, office buildings, service enterprises, and even country residences once occupied by Poland's landed aristocracy. One of these new would-be investors was Barbara Piasecka-Johnson, head of the Johnson & Johnson concern, who made a bid for the Gdansk Shipyard, an enterprise not only of immense significance as a symbol, but also one of the biggest shipbuilders in Europe. Another example was Anton Baranski, president of the Bustholz-Impolex hotel construction group.

With the fall of communist regimes in other East European countries the possibilities of investment in them began to be similarly explored by businessmen with ethnic connections with these lands. One such was Thomas Bata, principal shareholder in the well-known international shoe company. These new opportunities resulted in 1991 in the creation of dozens of new enterprises, the acquisition of equity in numerous formerly state-owned firms, and the commencement of negotiations on many other projects.

PURSUIT OF PROFIT

Maximization of profits is not, needless to say, a consideration alien to businessmen with East European backgrounds, but in many cases it is not their chief reason and often counts for far less than other motives, such as seeking prestige in the countries from which they hail, wishing to help their economies, etc. For other investors these are, of course, factors of scant significance and the direct financial return on an investment plays a far more important role. Analysis of experience to date seems to confirm that the search for direct high profits is beyond doubt the prime motive for investment in Eastern Europe by small and medium firms, but frequently only a secondary consideration for large companies.

The size of profits is closely bound up with the security of investment. In the communist period, meaning in effect to the end of 1989 (and in Bulgaria and Albania later still), any kind of profit projection was pointless since regulations (tax laws among them) kept changing and price movements were unpredictable. On the other hand, there was absolute certainty that a hungry market would absorb whatever was produced. The majority of foreign firms which had decided to invest made a point of planning operations in such a way that they could flexibly switch to new lines of production. This, of course, was not for reasons of marketing (since sales were assured), but of returns, since the profitability of different product lines was subject to constant change. Gross profit rates (before deductions for ploughbacks and taxes) tended to be huge, often coming to over 60 and, in many cases, even 100 per cent per annum. Even after payment of very high taxes and various other charges there remained a very sizeable balance. However, some enterprises made barely 'normal' profits of 10 to 30 per cent, which after liabilities left only a small residual accruing to the entrepreneur. Nevertheless, the average rate of return was very high. The problem was that it was an extremely theoretical one since there were a number of factors which in effect reduced it, two in particular:

1 the internal revenue departments' practice of taking several months to

inspect the annual balance sheets of foreign enterprises; pending approval of accounts, it was forbidden to make any dividend payments;

2 the high costs incurred by foreign enterprises in respect of all sorts of unofficial expenditures (including bribes to officials at various levels).

Even after allowing for these factors, payment of taxes, and so on, the net gains of foreign enterprises were often still very large. But then their owners ran into another obstacle: problems with repatriation of profits. To all intents and purposes they could only be remitted if they came out of exports, though even then that was not always easy. In the last year the situation in some countries has improved. In Yugoslavia, Hungary, Poland, and (since 1 January 1991) Czechoslovakia the domestic currency has been made internally convertible and can now be exchanged by enterprises for hard currency. However, some restrictions on remittances remained: in Poland, for example, at the turn of 1991 foreign enterprises were still allowed to transfer no more than 15 per cent of their profits (if they had no export earnings).

Some small businesses took their profits out illegally, converting them into hard currency in private bureaux de change. For bigger operations this avenue was, of course, impracticable and consequently exports were the only answer. In these circumstances foreign enterprises reacted in one of two ways:

1 Some decided, pending the expected relaxation in regulations, to devote their large profits to expansion through investment. The result was very rapid growth. Many small enterprises, which had gone into business in 1980–3 with less than 100,000 dollars in capital, posted turnovers in 1990 of over a million (and a few of over 10 million) and continued to expand.

2 Others decided to promote exports, which would enable them to transfer part of their profits. Since the profitability of exports of their own products to the West tended to be low, one of two solutions was adopted:

   (a) expansion of profitable exports to countries with non-convertible currencies (for instance, cosmetics from Poland and Hungary to the Soviet Union). The revenue could be used for the purchase in these countries of commodities which could then be sold profitably in the West (a wide range of secondary products such as mushrooms, bark, buttons, furs, etc.).

   (b) expansion in the countries in which they were based of departments which could yield export earnings. Since foreign enterprises are allowed to export only their own products, the adding of fictitious value to goods in demand in the West became a widespread practice. A good example is provided by the numerous foreign enterprises in

Eastern Europe which branched into the production of pallets: planks are bought from local timber yards, turned into makeshift 'pallets' with the help of a few nails, and exported. The Western customer removes the nails and has the planks he or she wants; the exporter circumvents the profit-transfer restrictions (and at the same time can claim an export tax allowance).

Since 1990 a new development has been observed in Eastern Europe following the decisions of governments to phase in tax systems similar to those in Western Europe and lift profit-transfer restrictions. Tax incentives for reinvestment will probably be introduced and the general rate of corporation tax is likely to be lower than in the European Community countries. The overhaul of the tax system is becoming increasingly necessary in view of Eastern Europe's rapid progress towards a market economy. In the countries furthest down this road – Poland, Hungary, and Slovenia – shop shelves are already full and in a growing number of fields a sellers' market is giving way to a buyers' on which it is becoming harder to dispose of goods. Foreign enterprises have an obvious advantage over indigenous competitors (state and private) since they can offer products tried and tested in the West and meeting the wants and tastes of East European consumers. Nevertheless, even the most dynamic of them will find in the new situation gross profit rates of over 50 per cent per annum increasingly rare and a level of under 30 per cent becoming the standard. On the other hand, lower taxes will mean a continuing high net profit rate.

There is another way of looking at this issue. The very high gross profit rates of foreign enterprises are chiefly attributable to two factors:

1 low labour costs;
2 high prices on the domestic market.

Seemingly, the effect of the inflation prevalent throughout Eastern Europe is to increase the prices of goods sold by foreign enterprises. But if they are measured in terms of inputs or converted into dollars, in many cases it will be found that in Poland, Hungary, Czechoslovakia, and Yugoslavia there has in fact been a substantial decrease. This has caused profit rates to fall in relation to those attained in preceding years. However, they still remain high on account of the low costs of labour. As shown in Figures 4.1 and 4.2 industrial wages in these four countries are several times lower than in Western Europe. This point is corroborated by the authors of studies of Eastern Europe. For instance, J.M.C. Rollo has written: 'The key attraction for foreign capital will be the high-quality work-force available at low wages.'[3] In the majority of industries the differences in the labour productivity of foreign enterprises are markedly smaller than the differences in

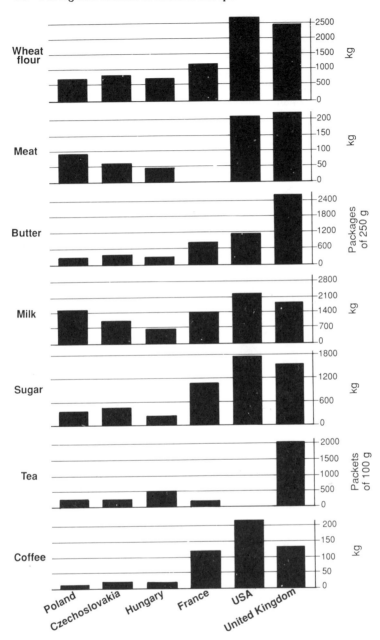

Figure 4.1 Equivalent of an average monthly salary in selected products in 1988

Source: Merril Lynch Report, *Rzeczpospolita*, 23 November 1990, p. 8

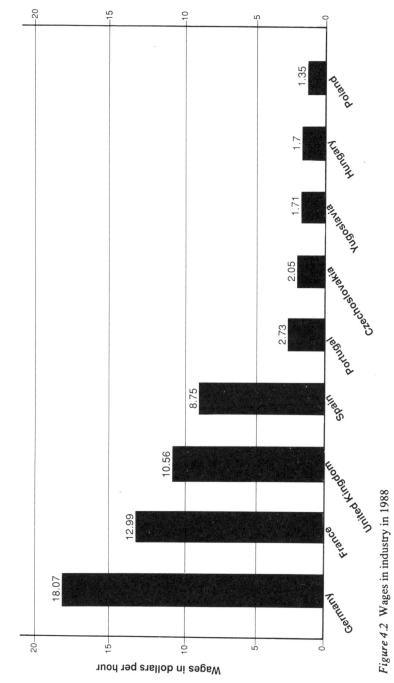

Figure 4.2 Wages in industry in 1988

Source: Maly Rocznick Statystyczny, Warsaw, GUS 1990, p. 274

wage levels, which naturally increases the profitability of investment and will be an inducement to a growing number of Western companies to move labour-intensive branches of production to Eastern Europe.

Some of the foreign enterprises which invest in Eastern Europe reap additional profits from certain other sources. One such is exploitation of their technological advantages. The transfer of more modern and efficient techniques and methods can be highly rewarding for dynamic enterprises in many fields of production and services.[4] Nor does this apply only to manufacturers of machinery, automobiles, and the like, since even a producer of good ball-point pens, for instance, will have an instant technological advantage in markets where poor quality predominates. The same goes for, say, insurance companies or retailing enterprises which bring to Eastern Europe the advantages of their long experience and modern work methods.

ENHANCEMENT OF THE POSITION OF ENTERPRISES

For big Western companies one of the basic considerations in deciding to invest in Eastern Europe is the possibility of augmenting the role played by them. Expansion of their sphere of operations through establishment of branches in Eastern Europe is now regarded by many leading Western companies as a key aspect of strategy, sometimes even more important than the immediate returns on capital. By way of example let us take the case of General Electric's acquisition of a stake in the Hungarian enterprise Tungsram.

A giant on the American market, General Electric had a much weaker position in Western Europe. In the light bulb business, crucial in terms of volume of turnover, its share of the West European market in 1989 came to only 2 per cent. Meanwhile, Tungsram was selling a large proportion of its light bulb production in Western Europe and had captured 7 per cent of the market (of its total annual sales revenues of 300 million dollars, 120 million were earned in Western Europe). In November 1989 General Electric bought a 50 per cent holding in Tungsram for the comparatively large sum of 150 million dollars. The financial returns on the deal were of less immediate concern to General Electric; the balance in 1990 will in fact come out in the red (earnings amounting to about 5 million dollars and additional capital expenditure to 20 million). Needless to say, General Electric cannot ignore the question of profit. With that in mind it has introduced numerous changes in organization, financial management, and employment in Tungsram which will in due course lead to an increase in direct financial profits. An additional benefit will be the transfer of a part of its research operations to Hungary where, it has been estimated, the expenditure involved will be about a fifth of the costs in the West.[5]

A slightly more rewarding transaction in financial terms will be the takeover by Asea Brown Boveri (known for short as ABB) of the Polish enterprises Zamech and Dolmel. ABB, Europe's largest electrical engineering group, first bought 75 per cent of the equity in Zamech-Elblag which is chiefly a manufacturer of electric turbines (the preliminary agreement was signed in February 1990) and then a majority holding in another Polish enterprise, Dolmel, whose product range includes turbogenerators and hydrogenerators.[6] The facilities of both are now being retooled and most of their output will be earmarked for export (which will be facilitated by the services of the ABB group). Within ABB's internal division of labour the Polish factories will be the sole producers of special turbines for energy-saving power plants.[7] Since the demand for turbines in Poland is now limited, production will begin of a containerized sewage treatment plant and state-of-the-art heating mains, both with a view to the Polish market. Through its investments in Poland the ABB group will significantly increase the value of its output (particularly of turbines) and also gain a foothold in the new and potentially interesting East European market. The direct financial net profits will be very small for the first three years in view of the capital expenditures required for modernization of the Polish factories, but in the long run could prove substantial.

A third example of investment undertaken in Eastern Europe chiefly with a view to the long-term strategic objectives of large Western companies and strengthening their position in the world is the automobile industry which will be discussed in greater detail in the next chapter. The big names in this field regard the countries of Eastern Europe as an element of business policy and are vying for control of its automobile industries for reasons of future expansion, competition with rival companies, and a larger share of European and world production. An important role is also played by hopes of the technical advantages to be gained from investment in Eastern Europe, such as the possibility of increasing the scale of production, so enabling stood-down models to be transferred at low cost, and a more rational division of labour in the manufacture of parts to be organized.

Such technical advantages are a source of economies of scale, and these in turn make for reductions of production costs and consequently increases in income.[8] However, these need not necessarily be earned in Eastern Europe. Both a strength and a weakness of large corporations is the fact that they pursue a global investment strategy in which the direct profitability of a project is often less important than other effects. The small direct profits yielded by an investment may be more than offset by its global benefits.[9] In the longer run this cannot of course mean the involvement of large companies in operations that are unlikely to pay; even ones that are treated as typical prestige projects are expected to show a profit.

CONQUEST OF NEW MARKETS

One of the natural, though sometimes unspoken, aims of the majority of large investment projects in Eastern Europe is the opening up of new markets. In setting up a new factory a large company has a guaranteed outlet for its machinery and a wide range of parts and components.[10] The same applies for the most part to takeovers of existing factories if they are followed by changes in technology and the product line. Investment in the distribution sector facilitates marketing, as does investment in other services. Small wonder, therefore, that recognition of Eastern Europe as an attractive new market could encourage many firms to invest. But is it really the case that Eastern Europe is a potentially huge market? Opinions are divided.

The current volume of East European imports is not very large. In 1990 it totalled a little under 100 billion dollars, which is approximately six times the level of Greek imports; on the other hand, it is barely half that of the United Kingdom. Economic change in Eastern Europe and in particular curtailment of state control of foreign trade, the gradual introduction of convertibility of national currencies, and privatization are hastening incorporation of its countries into the international division of labour. It can be assumed that in the short term their foreign trade will grow at a fast rate. It is harder, however, to draw longer-term conclusions. A report prepared by BIPE in France, IFO in Germany, Prometeia in Italy, and Cambridge Econometrics in Britain predicts that in the next few years 'the Eastern European market will exceed North America for the European Community economies'.[11] It is hard to predict whether the EEC exports to Eastern Europe will be higher than to the USA. However, it is not surprising that large enterprises operating in areas in which customers have to be competed for are loathe to let slip the existing opportunities and are contemplating entering the East European market. This is obvious in the case of invest- ments in car manufacturing which are tied up with supplies of machinery, parts, etc. Investors are also banking on the attachment of a part of the market to a particular trademark making it easier to sell cars built by the parent plant (e.g. Fiat in Italy). Even Ford has calculated that a relatively small investment in Hungary will facilitate sales of its product on the Hungarian market (in 1989 Hungary imported 200,000 cars, of which 12,000 were Fords).

One of the means by which foreign investors pursue the battle for the East European market is creation of their own distribution facilities. Many Western enterprises are now buying shops, department stores and warehouses and making strenuous efforts to build up their own retailing networks, which, apart from the immediate financial advantages, facilitates the marketing of their products. Some have concluded complex agreements. Kodak, for instance, is investing considerable funds in small photographic services outlets, which has resulted in a sharp rise in sales of its films and cameras.

In discussing Eastern Europe, we have a tendency to treat it as a single entity and use such terms as 'the East European market'. This is, of course, a major oversimplification: there is no such thing as a single East European market and there never has been, not even in the heyday of the Eastern bloc's economic grouping, the Council for Mutual Economic Assistance, better known as COMECON. The point is that the division of labour within COMECON had nothing to do with any kind of market mechanisms, but was based on inter-government agreements and decisions imposed by the Soviet Union on intra-East-European trade. There was no system of tariff reliefs. Exchange was once facilitated by the arrangements for mutual payments, but that ended on 1 January 1991 with a switch to settlements in convertible currencies.

The COMECON ceased to exist in August 1991 and its specialized agencies are now little more than a debating club trying to work out how to liquidate the assets of COMECON's defunct joint enterprises and institutions. That being so, what we are now looking at are seven discrete national markets varying greatly in size. Some idea of the degree of this differentiation can be gained from the gross national product of the countries in question (see Table 4.2).

The figures in Table 4.2 have to be treated with considerable reservation, since no way has yet been found of reliably computing the national product of East European countries. Be that as it may, they indicate that the GNP of the biggest of them, Poland, is twenty-six times larger than that of the smallest, Albania.

In view of both GNP levels and habits, price structures, etc. there are considerable differences between East European markets and those of, for instance, Western Europe. The countries of Eastern Europe represent, or soon will, a very large market for such products as computers, typewriters, microprocessors, certain drinks, watches, machinery and equipment for many types of small businesses (e.g. bakeries, butcheries, closing factories) or office supplies. But they represent a very small market for such products as equipment for the metallurgical, spinning and weaving industries or high-quality footwear. In many fields it is a specific market; for instance, the demand for small cars is relatively high, but very low, compared to Western Europe, for large and expensive makes.

Despite the absence of common mechanisms linking the markets of these seven countries, many foreign companies are investing in one of them as a springboard for penetration of the markets of its neighbours. There are

Table 4.2 Real gross national product in Eastern Europe, 1988 (in millions of dollars)

Country	GNP
Albania	13,200
Bulgaria	45,990
Czechoslovakia	115,750
Hungary	42,750
Poland	159,600
Romania	69,000
Yugoslavia	114,690

Sources: Human Development Report 1991, UNDP, New York, Oxford University Press, 1991, p. 119, and *World Bank Atlas*, New York, World Bank, 1989, pp. 6–9.

sound reasons for this: a shared history, a similar political and economic situation, and geographical proximity have developed certain ties which are also a significant factor in trade. Obviously, many producers will find it much easier to export to Eastern Europe from a base within one of its countries than from outside the region. To a certain, though much smaller, extent this also holds good for trade with the Soviet Union. East European enterprises' knowledge of the Soviet market, their personal contacts, and unconventional but effective methods of doing business can pave the way to making export dealings with the Soviet Union a properly commercial proposition.

It is worth observing that, though the products of Western firms (or their subsidiaries in Eastern Europe) enjoy immense popularity on a Soviet market starved of goods, the conclusion of contracts with Soviet importers is far from easy, and obtaining payment for deliveries more difficult still. Theoretically, Soviet enterprises are now autonomous and can import and export at their own discretion. In practice, however, they are allowed to retain for their own use only from 15 to 20 per cent of their hard currency earnings. This enables the Soviet state to conclude large-scale import contracts (grain purchases, for instance), but is an obstacle to transactions with other suppliers. In these circumstances, East European firms, with Polish ones leading the way, have mounted a vigorous marketing drive in the Soviet Union, partly as intermediaries. It is well exemplified by a trade fair organized in Minsk on 11–14 December 1990 by a Polish company, Perfect Agio, which was attended by 139 firms (including a number of joint ventures with foreign capital stakes). Each of them was allocated a tiny stand of 7 square metres. Thanks to a well-orchestrated publicity campaign, a host of potential customers were drawn to Minsk, many of them from very distant parts of the Soviet Union. Over 100 million dollars' worth of business was done, most of it in the form of barter deals. For instance, Abel, an Anglo-Polish joint venture based in Lublin, traded the products it was offering (which included Polish potatoes and carrots) for wine and grapes from Moldavia. Other firms obtained such goods as fuels (petrol and oil), timber, and gold. The barriers placed by the Soviet government in the way of barter trade were skilfully circumvented.

Sales on the Soviet market are also promoted by a swiftly growing network of agencies set up by East European firms under agreements concluded with individual republics which grant special facilities to certain countries; for instance, firms in Byelorussia in which a Polish partner has a stake of over 30 per cent enjoy a two-year tax holiday. Needless to say, these firms also deal in goods produced by other enterprises in their country.

These examples indicate the easier access to the Soviet market that could be exploited by companies investing in Eastern Europe. It must, however, be added that this does not apply to the whole range of goods, nor are there any guarantees as regards the future (the situation on the Soviet market is liable to sudden and radical changes). Another point is that enterprises in some East European countries (Hungary, Yugoslavia) have so far been unable to negotiate the kind of special facilities referred to above. In these circumstances, many investors focus chiefly on the market of their host country and on disposing of their products through their own sales network, for instance in West European markets.

The conventional theory of international economic relations propounds that foreign investment occurs if investors can obtain a higher profit rate off-shore than at home. This theory does not, of course, always hold good for projects carried out by entrepreneurs with a sentimental attachment to their ancestral countries. Studies indicate that higher profits may likewise not necessarily be the chief objective of big-name companies for which growth of the firm and prestige as well as various indirect forms of profit may be the basic consideration.

Distinguishing between the different reasons for investing in Eastern Europe is not always possible. Let us take the example of travel and hotel enterprises – and an increasing number of firms in these lines of business are now making serious approaches to the East European market. Investment in these countries undoubtedly forms part of their global strategy – so much so that for the leaders in the field not to own a hotel or agency in Eastern Europe is thought embarrassing. Its countries are rated poor markets: their nationals form a very small fraction of the clientele of

Western travel agencies and expensive hotels. On the other hand, the number of wealthy or well-to-do Westerners wishing to visit East European countries is growing by leaps and bounds. This is an inducement to building chains of new hotels.

Therefore, one can assume that there are a number of motives for investing in Eastern Europe. The main reasons are: pursuit of financial profits, enhancement of the position of enterprises, willingness to assure corporate growth, and penetration of newmarkets. Equally complex are the motives for investment in many sectors of industry.

5   Structure of foreign investment

The experience of other parts of the world has been that the structure of foreign investment is subject to considerable shifts over time.[1] These are due to changes in both regulations and profitability. For example, new regulations can ease restrictions on exploitation of mineral resources and so attract a flow of capital, but a decline in world commodity prices could halt the implementation of plans for mining industry investment. Another crucial consideration is the time factor itself. As we have noted in preceding chapters, large foreign companies tend to elaborate strategies for expansion into new areas with considerable deliberation, making numerous corrections from observations of the experience of other investors before they are prepared to undertake any major commitment of funds. Many widely publicized projects are aborted before they get off the ground; instead, new ones go ahead, often with a much lower profile. Because of these considerable changes in the structure of investment many of the following remarks, though they apply today, may be overtaken by future developments.

AGRICULTURE AND MINING

If we divide the economy into four sectors – agriculture, mining, manufacturing industry, and services – the present structure of foreign direct investment in Eastern Europe will appear simple: over 90 per cent is funnelled into manufacturing industry.

Theoretically, large-scale foreign investment in agriculture is feasible. In each country, including Poland, there are many big state farms of dubious viability which, because of the relatively low price of land, foreign investors would be willing to buy. This could lead to an increase in agricultural production. However, investment in agriculture is hindered by a general prejudice among the rural populations of Eastern Europe against the sale of land into foreign hands. Another obstacle is regulations which require purchases of land by foreign nationals or institutions to be approved by some branch of government (the Ministry of the Interior, for example). The net effect is that so far purchases have been very small.

A similar situation used to exist in mining, but in recent months it has altered significantly. Changes in internal price structures suddenly revealed that a large proportion of mines (coal mines included) were loss-makers. Plans have been drawn up for restructuring the industry, but they entail the closure of many mines, cutbacks in output, and redundancies. This has led to a change in the attitude of public opinion which until recently regarded natural resources as a good which had to remain under national control. Corresponding amendments are now being made in regulations. It looks as though the majority of East European countries will adopt the so-called 'Yugoslav model'. In Yugoslavia the law explicitly states that 'Private ownership of natural resources is not allowed. . . . The law permits the granting of a concession to a foreign investor for the extraction and processing of mineral resources, according to the Federal Law.'[2]

Investment by foreign enterprises in the mining industry has so far been limited. The biggest such project to date has been undertaken in Poland where in 1990 a joint venture, Pol-Tex Methane, was set up with the American company MacKenzie Methane and a Polish coal mine, Jastrzebie. Its purpose is extraction of the methane which occurs in large quantities (some 165 billion cubic metres) in the Rybnik Coal Basin in southern Poland. The new company has been promised a concession to explore and exploit the methane deposits of almost half the area in question. In the first stage of operations a relatively small investment of 16 million dollars will be made in thirty-six drillings, and it is hoped to begin industrial recovery by the end of 1991. If these expectations work out, the venture will then move into its second stage in which over 500 million dollars will be spent on drilling several hundred bore holes. The consequent output will make for a decided improvement in Poland's situation in the field of gas supplies (for which it has been almost totally dependent on imports from the Soviet Union). MacKenzie will pay all the costs of the project and be assigned 49 per cent of the equity (its share in the first year being as high as 85 per cent). Other companies, like Kelt Energie de France, have since followed in its footsteps and applied for licences to exploit methane and other gas deposits.

Another major investor is the American company Sulphurquest. It has entered into a joint venture called Sulphurquest of Poland which will spend 100 million dollars on the exploitation of sulphur deposits in a region close to the Soviet border.

In the long run, however, it is oil which will attract the biggest investment interest. Regulations as they now stand permit foreign companies to involve themselves in this industry in an operator capacity. Under contracts of this type, which are popular in many oil-producing countries, an investor concludes an agreement with an indigenous enterprise authorized to exploit mineral resources and act on its behalf but without property rights in the deposits. Such contracts are usually concluded in a situation in which the domestic enterprise is incapable (for financial, technological or organizational reasons) of operating on the scale required. Prospecting and exploration in the designated area is carried out at the foreign operator's own cost and, in effect, own risk. If deposits are discovered, they obtain exploitation rights (often to be negotiated in a separate agreement) for a specified period. The specific terms of each contract vary but, roughly speaking, boil down to operators obtaining in return for their investment a part of the output, the rest going to the indigenous enterprise or the state. In other words, for their considerable financial risk and outlay they are rewarded with only a part of the potential returns. Nevertheless, such contracts are willingly concluded by large oil companies and will probably also be found acceptable elsewhere in Eastern Europe.

Small quantities of oil have been discovered in all its countries and in each there is also some production (which in Romania at one stage even topped 10 million tonnes a year). Because of scarcity of funds and lack of equipment, the search for oil could not be carried out on a large enough scale, and there has as yet been no deep drilling in over half the region. This also applies to areas of sedimentary formation in which gas reservoirs have been found near the surface and petroleum could well occur at greater depths. It is likely that agreements will soon be concluded which will enable foreign companies to start explorations, especially as oil imports make up a substantial item in the trade balances of all of the East European countries with the exception of Albania. Discovery of new fields would bring them appreciable savings (see Table 5.1).

For Poland, Yugoslavia, Romania, and Bulgaria a wide-ranging search for offshore oil might also prove highly rewarding. Exploration with outdated equipment has already turned up numerous traces of petroleum (reservoirs have, for instance, been found on the Polish continental shelf, though their size is probably small). There is a real chance of the discovery of medium-size deposits that are relatively easy to exploit.

Gaffney, Cline and Associates have carried out an assessment of East European investment opportunities in the energy sector for the period 1990–2005. Even though certain realistic possibilities (such as exploitation of natural gas deposits in Bulgaria or Polish offshore petroleum deposits) were not taken into account, the figures given are high (see Table 5.2).

The mining industry also offers one other opening for investment: exploitation of the wastes that have accumulated over the decades.

Table 5.1 The cost of oil imports as a percentage of hard currency exports
calculated at prices per barrel

Country	Price per barrel		
	$10	*$20*	*$30*
Bulgaria	40	80	120
Czechoslovakia	30	60	90
Hungary	7	14	21
Poland	11	22	33
Romania	4	8	12
Yugoslavia	5	10	15

Source: J. Dempsey, 'Ailing Eastern Europe sails into an oil slick', *Financial Times*, 1990,
15 August, p. 16.

Table 5.2 East European investment opportunities to 2005 (in billions of Dollars)

Country	Oil	Gas	Coal	Pipelines	Refineries	Power	Total
Bulgaria	–	–	3	1	1	2–4	6–8
Czechoslovakia	–	–	12	1	2	2–3	17–18
Hungary	2	4	2	1	1	3–7	12–16
Poland	1	5–10	40–45	1	2	20–45	68–103
Romania	13	25	5	1	6	3–13	53–63
Yugoslavia	9	4	–	–	–	5–15	25–35

Source: *Prospects for and Opportunities in the East European and USSR Energy Markets to
2005*, London, Gaffney, Cline and Associates, 1990.

Extraction of mineral resources (zinc, lead, copper, bauxite, coal, iron ore,
etc.) has produced huge waste heaps which contain large quantities of
utilizable materials; bigger still are the slag heaps of steel works. The West
long ago developed technologies for the profitable (in some cases, such as
oil, copper, and silver, highly so) recycling of much of these wastes. There
are already certain established precedents for projects of this kind. In
Poland, for instance, there is a Polish–Hungarian company, Haldex, involved in the recovery of coal from mine tips. It now seems probable that
joint ventures with foreign enterprises for the exploitation of these reserves
are only a question of time. This would have the further benefit of helping
the natural environment.

MANUFACTURING INDUSTRY

Though it follows that foreign investment in extractive industries can be expected in the near future, they are not yet of any major significance. Investors' interest has so far been focused chiefly on some branches of the manufacturing sector.

The structure of foreign investment in industry has tended to be largely haphazard. The number of large or medium-sized factories built by foreign investors is still very small. For the most part, any major outlays have taken the form of purchase of equity (sometimes a majority holding) in existing enterprises, followed by their modernization. The choice available to companies wishing to buy into East European industry has been essentially limited. They have put up money for stock purchases and modernization only when this accorded with their long-term business strategy or was likely to yield exceptionally high returns. The majority of potential investors were unable to find the right kind of openings in Eastern Europe (for instance, electronics industry establishments were not put on the market) and consequently held back. This situation is now changing as a result of a broadening of the process of privatization in Eastern Europe.

There is far less haphazardness in the structure of small-scale foreign investment. Over 70 per cent of the projects undertaken in Eastern Europe involve the starting of small businesses. They have been launched in almost all sectors of the economy. The majority of small investors have built, sometimes as a joint venture with a domestic partner, new establishments, thanks to which they can choose their area of activity. The specific feature of the majority of these firms is that their production meets certain market shortages. A good example is the food and drinks industry. Investors have started production of articles which in a given country are either not made at all or made in too small quantities, for instance soft drink and fruit juice concentrates or attractively packaged sauces and seasonings; in the near future we can expect the formation of joint ventures in the field of canned beer and other drinks. Large global manufacturers of foodstuffs are creating their own networks of production and distribution facilities. In some cases this involves considerable expenditure. For instance, Coca Cola Poland is committed to investing at least 30 million dollars in 1991–2.

In the metal manufacturing industry there are now over 500 foreign enterprises in Eastern Europe producing for the most part small items of hardware (such as tools), but also, for example, housing elements and machine parts. In the textile and footwear industries there are another 500 foreign enterprises making women's wear, sports shoes, protective clothing, etc. Foreign investors have, however, so far tended to avoid such lines as yarn, fabrics, men's suits, and leather footwear on account of the considerable output of these articles by state industry. No doubt they will now seek to acquire controlling interests in some of the enterprises scheduled for privatization.

For some months serious negotiations have been under way regarding large-scale investment by foreign companies in Eastern Europe's chemical and petrochemical industries. This is largely connected with the situation on the oil markets of these countries. Until 1988 almost the whole of their demand (except for Albania and Romania) was met by cheap imports from the Soviet Union. Since then the latter has not only started cutting back supplies, but also switched to hard currency prices. This has forced its East European customers to reorient their petroleum procurement, and they are now importing, apart from crude oil, substantial quantities of petroleum products from the West. Construction of refineries by foreign investors would reduce this import bill. In the case of Poland, new refineries on its seaboard would also solve another problem: the shipment of oil. Most of the oil consumed in Poland is processed at Plock, a city in the centre of the country, and its transportation from terminals on the coast is very difficult. This is the justification for plans to construct a large refinery in the vicinity of the port facilities of Gdansk. It is worth adding that in terms of value one large refinery would cost more than all the foreign investment projects undertaken in Poland to the end of 1990.

Hitherto the biggest foreign investments have been made in the engineering and electrical industries. It is not infrequent for major companies to be the initiators of schemes for joint ventures with selected state enterprises, usually with a view to acquiring complete control of their assets (through purchase of over 50 per cent of their equity). In preceding chapters brief reference has been made to the American General Electric's investments in Hungary and the Swedish–Swiss Asea Brown Boveri's in Poland. Currently negotiations for takeovers of a large number of state enterprises in Eastern Europe are being conducted by several leading Western manufacturers of such goods as means of transportation (including tractors and ships), electrical household appliances, electronic equipment, and road-making and construction machinery. Though it is still too early for a precise determination of these companies' strategy, it is a reasonable assumption that it will be similar to that of the automobile corporations. Since the latter were the pioneers of capital expansion into Eastern Europe, have a detailed knowledge of its markets, and are contemplating further investment on a substantial scale, it seems useful to take a closer look at their business policy.

Some years ago, the communist leaders of Poland, Romania, Yugoslavia, and Bulgaria, realizing the backwardness of their countries' automobile industries, ordered domestic manufacturers to negotiate participation schemes with leading Western companies. Agreements were eventually concluded under which the latter supplied certain items of equipment, licences, and blueprints, in most cases on a buy-back basis. The results were highly unsatisfactory for both sides, but did lead to some progress in automobile production in Eastern Europe.

The political changes in this region have generated a sharp increase in Western car manufacturers' interest in Eastern Europe. In the battle for leadership in Europe and exploitation of economies of scale conquest of the potentially huge East European market will be a crucial factor. As Francesco Gallo, Fiat's executive vice-president for international activities, has explained:

> In Western Europe there is already strong competition in a fairly saturated market. With a growing Japanese presence it will become more and more crowded with a great effort needed to gain just a decisive point of market penetration. The big market of the future is Eastern Europe.[3]

As a result we are witnessing efforts by large corporations to establish bridgeheads in these countries from which to launch takeovers of car factories. In the early stages the most successful company has been Fiat which has two advantages:

1 a tradition of cooperation with East European countries;
2 low-price cars which are better suited to the purchasing power of East European customers than those manufactured by a majority of its competitors.

A series of new agreements have been concluded with Fiat by Poland and Yugoslavia. The latter is the only East European country in which Fiat has for a long time been a co-owner of the domestic automobile industry: in 1968 it acquired on a 'contractual joint venture' basis 18.5 per cent of the equity in Zavodi Crvena Zastava (ZCZ) in Kragujevac for 25 million dollars. In 1990 Fiat began negotiations for the purchase of a majority holding in ZCZ and guaranteed new investment.

In mid-1991 car factories in Poland were still state owned. Fiat is investing 770 million dollars in the FSM Bielsko-Biala plant. Under one of the new contracts Poland is to manufacture 160,000 Fiat Cinquecento (Micros) a year rising to 200,000. Mr Gallo claims: 'We could not produce 80–100,000 Micros a year in Western Europe at competitive costs, but 200–250,000 a year in Poland is economically viable'.[4] Another contract provides for substantial supplies of kits to the FSO Warsaw plant which is to make 120,000 Fiat Tipos.

An 'Eastern strategy' has also been framed by Volkswagen and Renault. Both companies already have factories in Yugoslavia. The Renault plant in

Novo Mesto in Slovenia has for a number of years been assembling the obsolescent R-4 for which there is still a market because it can sell at a price that undercuts the competition (though, in view of the 97 per cent purchase tax on cars in Yugoslavia, to describe it as cheap would be an exaggeration). In 1990 some 80,000 cars were built at Novo Mesto, and Renault plans to raise this to 150,000. For the most part these will be newer models, since the substantial profits accumulated in Yugoslavia are a handy source of investment.

The East European country which has latterly attracted the greatest interest on the part of Western auto manufacturers is Czechoslovakia. In the past its output was not particularly large, amounting to 193,000 cars a year, almost all of them produced by the state-owned Skoda enterprise. Though the machinery in its factories is antiquated and the cars made have engines of obsolescent design, foreign companies have formed a very high opinion of the skills of the local work-force. Skoda has a long tradition behind it, a fairly creditable record of exports to the West (45,500 cars sold in 1989, 16,200 of them in Britain),[5] and a positive balance sheet, despite selling at low prices. For foreign companies it could be not only a useful new 'bridgehead' in Eastern Europe, but also a cheap producer of parts and components for West European factories. Small wonder, then, that bids were made for Skoda by no less than twenty foreign companies. The field was quickly whittled down to only two: Volkswagen and Renault. Negotiations took up the whole of 1990. Renault's offer for a controlling interest was a capital investment of 2.5 billion dollars; Volkswagen pledged five billion. For fear of German dominance some Czechoslovak politicians favoured the Renault bid. The issue was further complicated by a demarcation dispute between the central government and the autonomous Czech government. However, economic arguments prevailed in the end, and in March 1991 the Czechoslovak government signed an agreement with Volkswagen.

The German company's Skoda deal is of historic significance for a number of reasons:

1 It is by far the biggest foreign investment agreement ever concluded in Eastern Europe;
2 It is also the biggest privatization operation undertaken anywhere in this region;
3 It represents a major victory for German business in the battle for East European markets.

Under this agreement Volkswagen will acquire a steadily growing share of the Skoda equity; from 31 per cent in 1991 to 70 in 1995. The remaining 30 per cent of the equity will be floated off eventually to private investors. In return for its controlling interest Volkswagen has undertaken to pay DM1.4 billion and to assure the investment of at least DM 9.5 billion (6.4 billion dollars). It will enable Skoda to raise output to 400,000 cars in 1997. Its engine manufacturing facilities will undergo even greater expansion, attaining by 1995 a capacity of 500,000 a year. Part of its production will be earmarked for exportation to other Volkswagen plants in Europe. Increased output will make it possible to avoid layoffs among the Skoda work-force. At present it employs 21,000 persons (15,000 of them in its Mlada Boleslavec factories). Since total employment is to remain at the same level as at present, this means that by 1997 output per employee will have risen at least 2.2 times. We are, therefore, looking at a huge leap in labour productivity.

Skoda will be run as an independent part of the Volkswagen group and the name will be retained alongside the VW, Audi and Seat marques. The Skoda dealer network in Europe will be expanded. For Czechoslovakia the Volkswagen agreement signifies a substantial increase in output and an even bigger one in exports. Moreover, other Czechoslovak enterprises have hopes of increasing sales to Skoda. For Volkswagen the deal with Skoda will 'strengthen its strategic position in central and eastern Europe. It [will] also enable VW to take advantage of the growth in the eastern European car market'.[6]

In May 1991, Volkswagen concluded an agreement with the enterprise BAZ. Volkswagen will own 94 per cent of shares in this enterprise. The BAZ factory near Bratislava will produce some 350,000 transmissions a year starting from 1994 and it will assemble some Passats.

Neighbouring Hungary has not hitherto been a car-producing country. The race for its market was won by Suzuki of Japan in October 1990 when the Hungarian authorities approved a joint venture with Autokonszern. The Japanese car maker got a 40 per cent stake in the new enterprise Magyar Suzuki and C. Itah (a Japanese trading group) 11 per cent. Suzuki will spend 175 million dollars on a plant for assembling cars, mainly from Japanese parts. Production is to start in 1992 with 15,000 cars and rise to a target level of 50,000 from 1995 onwards. Plans for an assembly plant, to be built in partnership with the Hungarian enterprise RABA, have also been announced by General Motors which wants to have it on stream by 1992, turning out 15,000 Opels and engines for export.

Another firm interested in Hungary is Ford. It will invest 80 million dollars in a factory producing automobile parts for export to Western Europe, chiefly ignition coils and fuel pumps. Bruce Blythe, Ford of Europe vice-president for business strategy, has said that the company's aim is to 'establish a world-class operation in Hungary, fully competitive in quality, technology and cost'.[7] The Hungarian government has agreed to grant Ford a ten-year tax holiday provided that the profits from the venture are reinvested. However, it seems unlikely that Ford expects any significant direct return on its Hungarian investment; the attraction lies in the prospect of supplies of cheap parts for its plants in Western Europe which will make them more competitive (in other words, indirect profits).

The unstable political situation in Romania and Bulgaria and the unpredictability of developments in Albania have resulted in little interest being shown in these countries up to the end of 1990 by major automobile and other companies. It seems, however, only a matter of time before the first two come to occupy a place in the global investment strategy of Western corporations.

The biggest market for the auto industry in Eastern Europe is Poland with 5 million registered passenger cars. The size of this market has aroused the interest of many companies; we have already referred to Fiat's successes in this field. Other companies, notably Renault of France and Opel of Germany, have also tried to enter into partnerships with Polish state enterprises. The prolonged and – on the Polish side – very ineptly conducted negotiations that followed discouraged potential investors (with the exception of Fiat). However, in late 1990, they resumed negotiations, but with smaller firms, for construction of assembly plants. Companies have since been formed which announced their plans to assemble small quantities of Chryslers in Bielsko-Biala and Korean cars in Bydgoszcz and Katowice.

The agreements already concluded will make for a significant increase in car production in Eastern Europe: from 1 million in 1990 to some 2 million by 1997. They will also have modernization spin-offs and improve competitiveness. They will, however, present these countries with the serious problem of reinforcing their automobile industries' technological and financial dependence on foreign companies guided by global policy considerations.

All the deals discussed so far relate to passenger cars. At the turn of 1991 no agreements had yet been concluded for the acquisition by Western companies of holdings in Eastern Europe's large truck and tractor industries. One of the difficulties is probably the fact that most of these factories also produce military equipment (such as tanks and armoured personnel carriers). But this is an obstacle that is likely to diminish with the passage of time and the way to joint ventures should then be clear.

BANKING, INSURANCE, CONSULTANCY

Though manufacturing industry will undoubtedly remain the chief area of Western capital expansion in Eastern Europe, there are a number of service sectors which are likely to be targeted in the near future, especially as the profitability of investment in services could be even greater than in the case of industry. Everything indicates that the same trends will be observed as in the rest of the world. In the early 1950s most foreign investment went into mining and resource-based manufacturing; services attracted less than 20 per cent. By the beginning of the 1970s this share had grown to 25 per cent and by the mid-1980s to 40 per cent.[8] It can be anticipated that in a few years services will account for as much as half the value of foreign investment. Though Eastern Europe's specific economic features are such that manufacturing industry will continue for a long time to come to be the principal magnet for investment capital, the role of services will grow.

Discussing foreign investment, Sir William Ryrie, executive vice-president of the International Finance Corporation, has written:

> How about service business? These are perhaps the biggest international opportunities. By definition, most services cannot be traded because they are consumed where they are created – at the hotel desk when a tourist checks in, for example. So as barriers to equity investment fall, services will take off.[9]

The vast and highly diverse sphere of services in Eastern Europe is not wide open to foreign investment. In the chapter on legislation relating to enterprises with a foreign capital stake we looked at the principal rules and regulations, and these of course have an equally crucial bearing on investments in services. However, there are many sectors which are also subject to specific regulatory measures which often narrow the possibilities of investment. This is the situation in, for instance, banking, insurance, telecommunications, and the media. Frequently, an even greater barrier, particularly in Romania, Bulgaria, and Albania, is the absence of regulations which effectively rules out investment in certain areas. However, the opportunities for foreign investors are gradually widening and new regulations, even if in some cases (for instance, television) very restrictive, give them greater scope and are arousing their interest.

But it also appears to be the case that there are certain areas of services which are of no interest at all to foreign investors, regardless of the legal position. One such is transportation. The number of companies which have invested in rail, road, sea, and air transport in Eastern Europe is very small, and the projects undertaken next to negligible. It is far from certain that changes can be expected in the near future in this crucial sector of the economy. There is also a lack of interest in such fields as health and education, even though there are no legal barriers whatsoever. More surprising is the very thin trickle of investment in the catering business, particularly fast-food restaurants.

Foreign investors are, therefore, concentrating only on certain services. One of them is banking. Projects in this sector are of importance not so much in terms of quantity (since the sums invested are unlikely to be very large in most cases) as of quality – in view of the role played by banks in economic life. Under communist rule it was in fact very limited, but that is being rapidly altered by the requirements of the reforms in Eastern Europe. These also make it necessary to overhaul the scope, methods, and style of banking.

A Polish foreign trade journal, *Rynki Zagraniczne*, has carried this assessment of the work of Polish banks:

> For visitors from the West the quality of the services offered is embarrassingly bad. It often takes a remittance several weeks to reach the provinces. Settlement of export and import payments sometimes takes even longer. Foreign currency deposited in one branch of a bank cannot be withdrawn in another branch, let alone another town.[10]

The same criticisms could in practice be made of the majority of banks throughout Eastern Europe. In these circumstances experienced foreign banks would have little trouble establishing themselves on the market of these countries. This would also be of benefit to Western investors as it would facilitate further expansion. However, because of the special role played by bank investment it is controlled by separate regulations which in effect put sizeable barriers in the way of wide-ranging operations by foreign banks.

Leading institutions in the banking field usually start out in Eastern Europe by opening agencies whose scope is very limited; above all, they are barred from performing deposit and credit functions. One example is Deutsche Bank which provides consulting services through offices in Poland, Czechoslovakia, and Hungary. It is likely that it will seek to establish a network of offices and eventually branches throughout Eastern Europe. Considerable initiative is also being displayed by French banks. Société Generale has opened offices in Bulgaria, Czechoslovakia, Poland, and Yugoslavia, operates through affiliated banks in Hungary, and has its own branch in Romania. Other French banks with a presence in Eastern Europe are Banque Nationale de Paris, CIC-UEI, and CCF. Other Western countries are represented by several tens of banks, among them Dredner Bank, Citicorp, NMB Bank of Netherlands, Banca Commerciale Italiana, Mitteleuropische N. Bank, and Privatbanken AS.

Several dozen Western banks have become shareholders in Eastern Europe's old banks or formed new ones in partnership with them. The latter include Nomura Investment Bank Hungary, set up in December 1990, in which Nomura holds 51 per cent of the equity and International Finance

Corporation 10 per cent, the remaining 39 per cent being held by the National Bank of Hungary and other Hungarian banks. In Poland there are a number of similar joint ventures, for example Bank Amerykanski w Polsce and Polsko–Szwecki Bank Kredytowy SCAN-Bank. The first bank with a foreign capital stake has also been opened in Albania, a joint venture with the Swiss company Iliria SA. Foreign investors have bought minority holdings in a number of partially privatized banks, but these are usually too small to give them any real say in policy.

Despite the apparently considerable number of foreign banks which have sprung up in Eastern Europe, their effective influence on the economy is still infinitesimal. Their turnover is also on the small side even though the opportunities are enormous. Among the most interesting potential sources of business for foreign banks are the remittances arising out of East European settlement or sojourn in North America and Western Europe. From immigrants or their descendants there is a flow of several billion dollars a year, a large proportion enclosed in letters as gifts to relatives in the old country. The money sent home by temporary residents, though hard to estimate, also adds up to a tidy sum and will grow rapidly with the relaxation of the immigration laws in Germany and some other Western countries. So far no one has given serious attention to this very substantial volume of money, only a fraction of which is or can be handled by indigenous banks since they have a very small network of branches in other countries. Channelling this stream of remittances would be of benefit to all concerned, though unquestionably a difficult operation (requiring, among other things, a suitable promotion campaign). Foreign banks have also been slow to move into other fields. Good prospects lie in exploitation of their technological advantages, for instance through the introduction of the automatic credit card systems unknown in Eastern Europe. No doubt, foreign bankers, a cautious breed by nature, are deterred by the risks.

The East European market is also of interest to Western insurance companies. The first of them appeared in late 1990 forming partnerships with indigenous institutions. These are the Polish–American Pierwsze Amerykansko–Polskie Towarzystwo Ubezpieczen na Zycie i Reasekuracji, SA (which handles life insurance) and the very similarly named Pierwsze Amerykansko–Polskie Towarzystwo Ubezpieczen i Reasekuracji, SA (other forms of insurance: accident, health, liability, automobile, credit, etc.). Fifty-five per cent of the stock in both cases is held by the American Life Insurance Company and AIV Insurance Company, the remaining 45 per cent by the Polish Bank PKO. Among rival ventures there is a Franco-Polish company in which Assurances Generales de France has a 49 per cent stake, the rest of the equity being owned by Polish foundations. Privatization of the insurance industry will create opportunities for Western companies to enter into partnerships with large institutions on a broader scale. But it is worth adding that in most European countries the regulations governing foreign investment in insurance are still far from clear; in Yugoslavia, for instance, such projects can only be undertaken as joint ventures with domestic partners.[11].

Western insurance companies have, however, been very active in Hungary. Generalli of Italy and Erste Allgemeine of Germany have bought into Allami Bizdosito, SA Colonia is part-owner of Atlasz, and SA Allianz of Germany has a 49 per cent holding in Hungaria Bizdosito.[12]

A very interesting and swiftly growing branch of services is consulting. In the majority of East European countries there are already hundreds of small domestic firms involved in this field, most of them with scant experience but large ambitions. Privatization and restructuring have created a huge demand for advisory services and among the major clients are foreign investors. In these circumstances numerous Western business consulting enterprises see a clear advantage in opening local offices. As Mike Lilley, one of the owners of the well-known British firm Ernst and Young, has explained:

> In Britain the rate is between 50 and 200 pounds. If our people go to Eastern Europe they can't in principle earn less. We realize that not everybody can afford it. So in Hungary our company Ernst and Young Bonitas has started training local experts. Since they live in Hungary their fees can be calculated according to the local cost-of-living index which is still much lower than in the West.[13]

At the end of 1990 Ernst and Young had four branches in Eastern Europe, in Hungary, Poland, Czechoslovakia, and Yugoslavia, its Hungarian office employing a staff of 120. The clients of such Western firms include both government agencies and foreign companies; on the other hand, little use has so far been made of their services by private firms in these countries. The service most frequently required by governments is valuation of enterprises and factories. Foreign customers seek guidance on 'the economic, financial and legal problems involved in setting up operations . . . help in negotiations, advice on taxes, expert opinions concerning the value of assets . . . market research [and] finding and selecting local personnel'.[14] Activity in the consulting field is also being vigorously pursued by local branches of foreign banks, either independently or on a cooperation basis.

So far consulting has focused chiefly (over 90 per cent of the business) on financial matters and general investment appraisal. But there can be no doubt that it has a much wider future and that one of the fields into which it will expand is technological know-how. This will in part be due to privatized enterprises' need for advice on such matters as low-cost but efficient modernization of their capacities, product innovation, utilization of new materials, etc. An equally important factor will be the implementation of increasingly complex projects, such as development of industrial zones (or parks) and trade centres. This will create a demand for the services of consultants with special skills and the ability to work with local partners.

TRADE

The area in which the largest number of projects have been undertaken in the services sector in Eastern Europe by foreign investors is trade. The majority of these investments have gone into retailing. They are of a highly diverse nature. There are numerous shops which belong to firms involved in industrial production in Eastern Europe. These shops sell the products made by their owner, but in order to attract custom and increase sales many of them also offer goods supplied by other firms. New regulations allow them to do so. A good example of how this has worked is Johnson & Johnson of the USA, a household name in pharmaceutical and hygienic products. In July 1989, seeing the changes in the wind, it opened a small office in Warsaw to promote sales to the state-owned retailing network. The law as it then stood prohibited the sale of imported products directly to the market. In January 1990 the law was changed, and Johnson & Johnson promptly transformed its Warsaw office into a limited stock company for the purpose of importing the products of the parent company and selling them directly to drugstores, supermarkets, and hospitals. The change in the regulations has also meant that products can be delivered much more rapidly. The abrupt increase in marketing opportunities has led Johnson & Johnson to buy a large warehouse and engage intermediaries to distribute its products.

Though John R. Bachman, general manager of Johnson & Johnson (Poland), has complained of the difficult working conditions in Poland, above all, the 'infamous telecommunications system', he also stresses the expansion possibilities in a country with a population of 38 million. 'It's a new market, with very small penetration. So there's a tremendous opportunity for growth.'[15]

One of the pioneers of comprehensive penetration of the East European market is Puma, the well-known German sportswear manufacturer. It has entered into cooperation arrangements with enterprises in a number of East European countries and also started production in factories which it co-owns. Yugoslavia and Hungary have now become major producers of Puma's products; so, too, though on a smaller scale, have Czechoslovakia, Bulgaria, and Poland. These products are marketed through Puma's own retailing network which has been growing very rapidly: in Poland, for instance, where the first shop was opened in 1989, it quickly created a chain of as many as 250 by the end of 1991 (including a number belonging to another foreign company, Randall, which has a special agreement with Puma). The East European market is also, if somewhat late in the day, being entered by Puma's principal competitor, Adidas, whose management is building up a network of outlets in most of these countries. A substantial proportion of the merchandise will be the products of local factories owned by other firms (including some in the state sector) made to Adidas specifications.

These examples illustrate the diversity of the forms of expansion by foreign companies. Most of them have one thing in common: promotion of their own brands. Another form of commercial expansion, also geared chiefly to sales of a firm's own products, is being put into effect by Kodak. At a very small outlay in direct investment it is concluding contracts with a growing number of owners of the various kinds of outlets which develop and sell Kodak films and cameras. Such contracts have been concluded with photographers, shopkeepers, and even newsagents. As a result a dense distribution and service network is being developed which will ensure Kodak a rapid growth of sales.

Kodak's services network is working according to the principles of franchising. The same can be said about many other trade networks, like Kleider Bauer, Yves Rocher, Benetton, and also about fast-food networks. The first McDonald's restaurant was opened in Belgrade some years ago, a second one in Budapest in 1988. Pleased at the success of its Budapest Vaci Utca restaurant, McDonald decided to look for franchise partners to open more. To its surprise, hundreds replied to the advertisement, many with enough capital to pay the licence fee of 4.3 million forints (57,000 dollars). At the end of 1992, the McDonald network in Hungary will probably comprise some twenty restaurants. When Fast Food Systems International advertised franchise licences in Hungary for its Dixie Fried Chicken restaurants, it got the same overwhelming response. Other firms that have completed contracts include Burger King, Pizza Hut, Budget, Avis, Landauer.[16]

Foreign investors are also interested in acquiring controlling stakes in privatized department stores. This process began in Hungary where a number of large establishments have been taken over by foreign companies, and has since spread to Poland, Yugoslavia, and Czechoslovakia. The usual objective of such acquisitions is profit, both direct and indirect (through sales of products from the factories of the stores' new owners), but in some cases direct profits have been a secondary consideration. An example of an operation in this latter category is the takeover of the 'Saturn' department store in Torun (Poland) by Bresse-Pol, a newly formed company of which

60 per cent is owned by French agricultural cooperatives in Ain department store and the rest by Polish shareholders. It was the first Polish department store to be privatized. The French investment was small – under 2 million dollars – and for the first four years all profits are to be reinvested locally. Some 15 per cent of the store's turnover consists of French products, mostly from the cooperatives which are the majority shareholders.

A different kind of venture is the Gdansk–Hamburg Investment and Trading Company, in which 51 per cent of the equity is owned by IMG Immobilien und Beteiligungsgesellscahft mbH of Germany, 34 per cent by other German investors, and 15 per cent by the Polish state-owned Voivodship Internal Trade Enterprise. This company has leased (for, as it happens, the peppercorn rent of only one dollar per square metre) the 'Sesame' department store in Gdansk and has been netting very large profits, largely from sales of German-made products. Nor can it have been bad for the business that one of the directors of the company was at the time of its establishment the chief executive officer of the voivodship (regional) government authorities, a circumstance given wide exposure in the Polish press.[17]

Takeovers of existing department stores are not always feasible: in any case, their number is too small and they are often badly situated. In these conditions streams of proposals have been coming for the past months from promoters of developments of modern shopping centres organized along Western lines. Once again, Hungary, Poland, and Czechoslovakia have been the chief focus of interest. The first such projects have been located in or beneath foreign-operated hotels; they will be followed by shopping malls in central city areas. Since there are certain to be increases in municipal taxes and a boom in downtown property prices, it is likely that in the near future similar precincts will also spring up on the outskirts of large cities, as is happening in a number of Western countries.

Schemes for foreign investment in new commercial developments are in most cases welcomed by central and local governments. However, they are not always plain sailing, new obstacles being continually put in their way at all levels by a bureaucracy intent on protecting old structures and unwilling to promote system changes. Another hurdle is that senior officials are not always able (or willing) to understand the basic rules of the world of business. This point is illustrated by the history of the 'French village' project, a development embracing shops, a theatre, a cinema, and a sports centre which a French group wanted to build in Warsaw or its immediate environs. After months of negotiations they came away empty handed. Time lost is, of course, money lost; nevertheless it is safe to say that foreign investment will grow and become a factor with an increasing impact on internal trade in Eastern Europe.

Foreign investors are also making takeover bids for enterprises involved in external trade. One example is the Hungarian state enterprise Inter-cooperation. In 1989 it was bought by the international Gertz Corporation, a trading unit of the Marmon group of companies.[18] Through this acquisition Gertz has obtained access to markets in Africa and South-East Asia as well as Eastern Europe.

Another example of such investment in external trade is the sell-off of the Polish enterprise Universal. The privatization of this foreign trade agency was carried out in 1990, with 30 per cent of the equity being offered to foreign companies. The latter will no doubt seek in due course to increase their holdings when shares become tradeable on the stock market.

COMMUNICATIONS, TOURISM, AND OTHER SERVICES

The majority of foreign businessmen, when asked about their most trying experiences in Eastern Europe, will point to telecommunications, and above all telephone services. Unfortunately, their complaints are largely justified. Long and often futile waits for long-distance calls, problems with automatic dialling, crossed lines, poor audibility, and the like are a serious obstacle to efficiency and expose foreign investors to losses. Of course, some solution can always be found; for instance, in many cities with poor telephone systems fax machines somehow manage to work. In the long run, however, investment in telecommunications is indispensable. Since the needs of East European countries are immense, we have for over a year been witnessing an invasion of potential investors offering partial remedies for these problems in return for concessions. Among them are both large companies, such as Ericsson of Sweden and AT&T of the USA, and smaller operations, such as Crowley Cellular Telecommunications, Alcatel of France, and others.

For some time investment was impeded by the regulations in force or an absence of them. However, this situation is gradually changing as new legislation comes into effect in each East European country which facilitates foreign investment in telephony and other means of communication. This has enabled joint ventures to be launched for penetration of the East European market, and not only on the operating but also on the production side. For instance, in October 1990 Alcatel and a group of Polish enterprises formed a company, Alcatel Cit Polska, which is building telephone exchanges (production is expected to reach the equivalent of 300,000 numbers by 1994). In Hungary manufacturers of telecommunications equipment have even obtained special tax reliefs.

Most of the telephone and fax requirements of foreign companies will soon be met, and they will be provided with efficient international services (at special rates close to the West European level). However, taking a realistic view, it is hard to share the assumption made by optimists that foreign investment will quickly solve the problem of backwardness in the telecommunications field on a national scale. The needs are enormous; it is estimated that Eastern Europe lacks 20 million telephones (with pessimists putting the shortage at 30 million). That would call for investment many times larger than currently planned.

The new legislation on foreign investment in telecommunications tends to make an exception of the most profitable area, that is telephone connections with abroad. In Poland, for instance, a law passed in October 1990 permits them to be provided solely by Polish firms or joint ventures in which the foreign stake does not exceed 49 per cent of the nominal or share capital. In Yugoslavia, under the 1988 Foreign Investment Law (Article 21), investments in telecommunications can only be made by domestic enterprises and companies in which there is a Yugoslav holding; this restriction still remains in force.

The new regulations also open the way to demonopolization of posts and telegraphs, but this is a channel of communications in which foreign investors have so far shown little or no interest. The mass media – the press, radio, and television – are a totally different matter. This is due to the special role of investment in these fields: they are regarded as exceptionally profitable, mainly on account of the advertising revenue, and a means of influencing the tastes and habits of the public. Control of mass media is also a factor of immense political significance, a consideration that has led East European countries to adopt a very cautious approach to the sale of newspapers and broadcasting stations to foreigners. A contributing reason is the Hungarian experience.

In Hungary foreign investment in the mass media was treated on a par with investment in any other part of the economy. In the first months of 1990, in the favourable circumstances arising out of the disintegration of the communist system in 1989, foreign investors managed to buy at knockdown prices a sizeable slice of the Hungarian press. Even the biggest national dailies like *Magyar Nemzet*, *Nepszabadsag*, and *Magyar Hirap* were transformed into joint ventures in which Western firms held a controlling interest. The biggest stake was acquired by Germany's Springer group.

Until 1989 the majority of the biggest newspapers and magazines in Eastern Europe were directly controlled by the communist party and its acolytes (such as the so-called 'national fronts'). Most of them were then placed by the new governments under the caretaker administration of a commission or some other body specially appointed to supervise the process of their privatization. In practice this means that papers with the largest circulation are now assigned to indigenous *ad hoc* syndicates, including organizations of various kinds formed by their staffs. In these circumstances the openings for foreign investors are limited to only a small number of truly important titles. Takeover bids are made chiefly by publishers with a long-term strategy for penetration of the East European market. The most active are Axel Springer, Hersant (Socpresse) and Rupert Murdoch who seem to be aiming at building up their own newspaper chains in each of these countries.

An increasingly frequent practice is for newspapers to be put up for auction. A situation in which the number of political parties competing for power in Eastern Europe is growing and each seeks to acquire its own organ is, of course, rapidly boosting the market price of newspapers. Since higher prices generally mean lower investment profitability, foreign companies are considering the possibility of creating new publications, an idea once rejected, but now becoming increasingly popular. The first ventures were magazines for children and juveniles, comics, and pornography. In late 1990 there also came the first attempts by foreign investors to launch new dailies and quality journals.

There are no barriers to the acquisition of minority holdings in newspapers. However, this is a form of investment that has so far had few takers. Portfolio investors are put off by the degree of risk involved, while Western publishing concerns are not interested in investments which do not give them control of the paper they are buying into (or at least a fifty–fifty split of the stock ensuring them an effective voice in its affairs).

In the case of the broadcasting media such a situation is still impossible in most of the East European countries. In Poland the law of 28 October 1990 permits licences to operate radio and television transmitters to be granted only to wholly owned Polish companies or ones in which the foreign stake does not exceed 33 per cent of the nominal or equity capital. Private television companies are required to pay their own way; in other words, they are not entitled to a share of licence fees (which means that their basic source of revenue has to be advertising). In spite of all these restrictions, the possibility of investment in broadcasting media has aroused considerable foreign interest, especially in view of a point made by Ms Teresa Kaca of the legal department of the Polish Ministry of Communications:

> Taking part in the administration of a broadcasting station, including having a decisive say, is a question of agreement. The business code allows for the possibility of having the partners decide on how the responsibility is to be divided, and also who is to have what control over programmes – so that this can be done in a different way than in proportion to the capital input.[19]

Almost overnight the Ministry received about a hundred offers from potential foreign investors.

It is worth pointing out that in countries in which the regulations governing foreign investment in broadcasting media are liberal, actual practice tends to be restrictive. In Yugoslavia, for instance, such investment is barred only to companies wholly owned (100 per cent of the stock) by foreigners, but is theoretically open to joint ventures with a foreign holding of anything up to 99 per cent. However, that is only in theory; in practice permission for any such projects is regularly denied by the government.

The restrictions on foreign investment in broadcasting do not, needless to say, extend to the distribution of programmes. As a result, efforts are now being made by foreign companies to develop the cable and satellite television market. Numerous joint ventures have been launched in the field of satellite television installations, at first for individual households, but now also on a pooled basis. Investments on a larger scale are usually joint ventures by foreign companies, which supply most of the equipment and meet the hard currency expenses, domestic enterprises, and local authorities.

The biggest contract of this kind to date has been concluded by an enterprise called Poland Cablevision which is registered in the Netherlands and jointly owned by David Chase (the Polish-born head of the American Chase Manhattan Bank), the Polish Post Office, and Polish Radio and Television. They have formed a company, Polish Cable Television, in which Poland Cablevision has a 70 per cent stake and which plans over a three-year period to install cables in all the bigger buildings of the eastern city of Bialystok for the reception on a monthly subscription basis of some thirty satellite TV programmes. The costs of this project – some 300 million dollars – will be met by Chase. In 1991 Polish Cable Television drew up a programme for expansion of its network to Warsaw, Cracow, Wroclaw, Katowice, Gdansk, Szczecin, and Bydgoszcz. Agreements have been pencilled in with the mayors of these cities. The estimated costs of the whole investment come to 800 million dollars.

A segment of the economy which has been *par excellence* a domain of foreign investment is hotels and tourism. For dozens of years the tourist trade has been booming all over the world, and its economic and social role is growing steadily. As in the case of industry, investment in this field has a multiplier effect. Building a hotel which is to provide accommodation for foreign tourists usually produces spin-offs in the form of new restaurants and coffee-shops, more business for shops, additional employment for taxi-drivers, etc. These phenomena can also be observed in Eastern Europe.

As we have seen in an earlier chapter, the hotel business was a market penetrated by foreign enterprises long before 'normal' investment in

Eastern Europe became possible. At the turn of the 1980s the capitals of most of these countries had several large hotels built and temporarily administered by foreign enterprises, though owned by the state. These were highly profitable deals for both parties. In Poland the principal domestic partner in such projects was the state enterprise Orbis. Between 1973 and 1985 twenty-six hotels were built for Orbis by foreign investors. How big a return the latter got for their money is not on record; what we do know is that Orbis paid off the last instalment of the 410 million dollars it owed for the construction of these hotels in 1988 and thus became their sole owner. In the same period the state collected 650 million dollars in taxes from Orbis.[20] Investments of this type are still being undertaken, though on a diminishing scale, since it now makes better economic sense for investors to own the hotels built by them. This has become possible in the last two years.

The issuing of regulations permitting foreign investment triggered a sudden increase in the interest of large Western tourist enterprises in the possibilities of hotel construction in East European countries. The governments of the latter were equally interested since the scarcity of overnight accommodation was not the least of the barriers to the expansion of external economic relations. Loud complaints were also voiced by businessmen for whom the hotel situation was a particular bugbear. Accommodation was reserved for package tours and privileged citizens; ordinary customers were treated as nuisances. For seasoned travellers to Eastern Europe this was no problem: they had learned that the incivility of hotel staff and 'No Vacancies' signs could be cured at a stroke by a handful of discreetly proffered dollar bills. It was not unknown for such a 'regular' to obtain a room at the expense of some other foreign visitor who had made a booking and naively supposed that this was enough.

The immense demand for hotel accommodation on the part of businessmen, representatives of international organizations, and other expense-account travellers now flocking to Eastern Europe has generated new investment. In 1991 the majority of its capitals and certain other cities of major economic importance had big hotels belonging to well-known hotel chains. Most of them are new and some very large indeed. Their operators have managed to ensure a standard of service close to that found in high-class hotels in Western Europe. Special telephone links with cities in other countries have been installed, which has removed one of the most troublesome hindrances to doing business in Eastern Europe.

There is, however, another problem which has not been solved: development of services for ordinary tourists. Foreign investment in this sphere was to a large extent channelled into takeovers of existing hotel facilities. The pioneer was Hungary where, as we shall see, foreign investors have acquired part of the assets of the Ibusz tourist enterprise. Privatization of other operations in the hotel and travel business has also started: Hungarhotels, the Danubus Hotel and Spa Company, and the Pannonia Hotel and Catering Company. Foreign companies have bought minority holdings in a large number of Hungarian hotels; according to optimists, services have improved as a result. A similar trend can be observed in Poland where foreign investors are buying into privatized hotel enterprises.

Without a doubt, privatization, foreign investment, and greater competition are a spur to better hotel services. Various illogical and frustrating regulations are gradually being weeded out and replaced by normal financing principles. The most glaring aberrations are becoming a thing of the past. A good example of the kind of bizarre practices that until recently were a feature of Eastern Europe was the pricing system in the large Victoria Hotel in one of its capitals. In 1989 a room there cost 134 dollars per night, but a 'special discount' was offered to foreigners which reduced the price to about a hundred dollars. However, to obtain it they first had to send fifty dollars to the state enterprise to which the Victoria belonged in order to enquire if the hotel had rooms available at this lower rate. If there were no such vacancies the fifty dollars were refunded.[21]

Improvements in the functioning of some of the older hotels will unquestionably be a boost to Eastern Europe's external relations. It is, however, worth remembering that in most of them such improvements have not yet come about. Nor has something else that was also expected: the building by foreign investors of any significant number of new hotels away from capital cities and the biggest industrial centres. Such projects are still very rare. Thousands of plans have been drawn up, but difficulties arise in getting them off the drawing board. This is partly due to bureaucratic sloth and the frequent lack of regulation of the question of land property rights. Investment proposals take months to consider and agreements once concluded (e.g. between a company which wants to invest and a municipal authority) are liable to be questioned by some other authority (at a superior level, for instance). Similar problems may, for that matter, be encountered in the big cities as well; their solution has not been eased by the devolution of greater powers to elected branches of local government. A case in point was the proposed construction of several large hotels in the centre of Warsaw. Hyatt, Pulmann, CBC, and other groups applied to the metropolitan authorities for land and were provisionally offered a site in a good location. The terms of the deal were also pencilled in: the Warsaw authorities undertook to contribute the land, the foreign partners were to build the hotels, and the profits were to be shared. But the road from preliminary agreement to construction has proved to be a long one. In November 1991 negotiations, which began in 1989, were still continuing.

In fairness it has to be added that in some smaller towns the whole procedure has been completed in a matter of weeks. In other East European countries the situation is similar. Though the financial losses suffered by potential investors are not great, the inordinate amount of time spent discussing projects consumes energies; nor does it by any means make it easier to solve future financing problems.

In due course obstacles of this kind will no doubt be eliminated. The countries concerned incur losses as a result of the delays in projects, some potential investors become discouraged and back out, but others proceed regardless. In the next few years new hotel complexes will also be developed in attractive tourist regions: the Adriatic in Yugoslavia, the Black Sea and the mountains in Bulgaria and Romania, the Tatras in Czechoslovakia, the Lake Mazury and forest district in Poland.

Construction of upmarket hotels by big-name international chains will provide a magnet for affluent visitors from the West. A mass influx of ordinary tourists could be advanced by another type of activity: the creation of well-run travel agencies with good international connections. Eastern Europe already has a sizeable quantity of small and medium-size hotels which are now being privatized. Far larger is the number of unofficial pensions: private houses which rent rooms to tourists. The guests are denied such amenities as television (rooms are not equipped with TV and there are no clubrooms), guidebooks, etc. The first foreign agencies which manage to enter into permanent arrangements with the owners of these unofficial boarding houses, and persuade them to guarantee certain minimum standards of comfort, will undoubtedly find handsome profits there. These agencies will have to cooperate with local firms, whose lack of experience is offset by their knowledge of the local situation. These may go to such organizations as ACCOR of France which is dotting Eastern Europe with its own network of hotels (in Poland alone it has already opened six Novotels).

Summing up, we can say that the sphere of investment activity by foreign enterprises in Eastern Europe is expanding swiftly. In terms of size of financial outlays projects in manufacturing industry decidedly lead the way, but we are also witnessing a rapid growth of expenditure in other segments of the economy, even in such fields as mining and television. On the other hand, there are many areas where there has been little or no foreign investment. These include agriculture, a large part of heavy industry, and transportation. The structure of foreign investment will continue to change, mainly in the wake of progress in privatization.

6   Geography of foreign investment

Because changes in the quantity and directions of foreign investment in Eastern Europe are so mercurial and the difficulties involved in recording its true dimensions so great it will be some years before complete and reliable data on its scale and structure are available. However, we do have information about the investment plans of new foreign enterprises. In each of the countries concerned newly formed enterprises are required to notify the appropriate government institution of their development plans, enclosing a financial breakdown of their investment programme. Of course, the actual capital expenditures and the figures given in these programmes will vary significantly. The real structure of foreign investment can only be delineated on the basis of projects completed, and in the present conditions the size of these is in most cases impossible to establish. It also has to be said that there tend to be marked variations between the official figures available from different sources (for instance, the foreign investment agency and the finance ministry of one and the same country). These qualifications must be kept in mind when considering the information that follows, even though most of it comes from official sources.

COUNTRIES OF ORIGIN

Over 70 per cent of foreign direct investment in the world as a whole is accounted for by five countries: the United States, the United Kingdom, Japan, Germany, and France, though there are certain variations in its actual structure from one part of the world to another. In East and South-East Asia, for instance, pride of place belongs to Japan. In Eastern Europe the deviations from the world pattern are even greater: among the principal investors there are countries like Austria and Italy, while Japan has so far played a very minor role.

Any statistics concerning the distribution of foreign investments by country of origin has to be seen as appropriate. We have to remember that some enterprises investing in Eastern Europe belong to holdings from other countries, for example the German company Opel is controlled by the American company General Motors. Some Austrian-registered enterprises are filials of holdings from Germany, USA, and UK. However, in a great majority of cases investments in Eastern Europe are, at least until now, executed directly by 'mother' enterprises (enterprises registered in the countries of origin of the majority of capital).

Everywhere in Eastern Europe with the exception of Albania the list of countries of origin is a very long one. In the case of Poland, Hungary, and Yugoslavia it amounts to over thirty. However, closer scrutiny reveals that throughout the region over 90 per cent of foreign investment comes from less than ten countries.

Another characteristic feature of the situation in Eastern Europe is the exceptionally small flows of capital between the countries of the region. In Western Europe neighbouring countries account for a large proportion of foreign investment. The same is even true of the United States where Canadian and Mexican capital is heavily committed. In Eastern Europe, on the other hand, investment by enterprises from adjoining countries has so far been very scant, even after making due allowance for their limited capacities. It is in fact many times smaller than these enterprises' investments in the West. In the popular view the explanations for this are largely very mundane, one of them being the fact that prior to 1990 trips to the West for managers of state-owned enterprises in Eastern Europe were an infinitely more attractive and rewarding proposition than trips to the East. Privatization and the pursuit of profit have altered the perspective of the enterprises, which makes it likely that a rapid growth of offshore investment within Eastern Europe is imminent.

Very small, too, are the dimensions of investment by enterprises from the developing countries. Most of the plans (with respect, for instance, to capital from the oil-producing nations) came to nothing. Though it is true that a large number of firms have been started in Eastern Europe by Third World nationals, these are on the whole very small businesses, their proprietors often being people who studied in a particular country or political refugees.

Over 90 per cent of foreign investment in Eastern Europe comes from the OECD countries. In Poland, Hungary, and Yugoslavia, for example, firms from over half of them are involved in various projects. This apparent geographical diversification of the origins of capital is, however, misleading. All the material to hand indicates that throughout Eastern Europe the biggest role is played by one country: Germany. It has to be added that as a general rule German enterprises have a better knowledge of the East European market and are usually quick to make the most of the existing opportunities.

The successes of German enterprises have been facilitated by such factors as:

1 geographical proximity;
2 the prominent place occupied by Germany in Eastern Europe's foreign trade;
3 the co-production deals concluded by large West German companies with enterprises in Eastern Europe in the 1970s;
4 the historical tradition of German capital expansion into the region in question.

Among the nations of Eastern Europe German capital expansion is a source of both the greatest fears and the greatest hopes. People fear the possibility of dependence on Germany and what are often only the incidental effects of German capital expansion. But at the same time the launching of production in their countries by companies with established reputations is greeted enthusiastically. Without a doubt, a general belief in the quality of German production and the reliability of German firms has helped to clear the path for investment.

The German business world is also better prepared than its competitors for expansion. Any new regulations issued by an East European country are instantly translated and analysed by German companies, research institutes, and government agencies, and if faults are found with them these are made known without delay to the government and opinion leaders of the country concerned. The implementation of investment projects is facilitated by German banks which have opened offices in the majority of East European capitals. The efficiency of German operations is augmented by the support received from the country's energetic embassies and the numerous international agreements concluded by Germany with East European countries.

In Poland another boost to expansion has come from the establishment in November 1990 of a German Economic Representative's Office. The initiative came from three organizations: Deutscher Industrie und Handelstag, Ost-Ausschuss der Deutschen Wirtschaft, and Bundesverband der Deutschen Industrie. This agency provides German companies with information and advice on investment opportunities and joint projects and looks after the interests of investors.

In Yugoslavia, where the door to foreign investment was opened earliest, 22 per cent of all such projects in 1968–88 were of German origin. In subsequent years the role of German capital grew bigger still. In 1989 it accounted for 26.5 per cent of foreign investment.[1] In 1989 and 1990 no less than 700 new firms with a German capital stake (including some that are wholly owned) were launched in Yugoslavia. Among the companies operating on the Yugoslav market are Siemens, Volkswagen, AEG-Telefunken, and Hoechst.

In Hungary there were forty-eight German joint ventures in April 1989 and 1,400 in January 1991. They amounted to 36 per cent of the total number of projects of this kind and accounted for 30 per cent of the capital of all foreign enterprises.[2] As in the case of other East European countries, appraisal of the value of the investments actually undertaken is still impossible.

In Poland, German companies have been in the forefront from the outset. Of the fifty-two joint ventures approved to the end of 1988 seventeen had German capital stakes. In mid-1990, out of a total of 1,538 joint ventures, German capital was involved in 616, in other words in over 40 per cent of all companies. However, the qualification has to be made that Germany's share in the whole of foreign investment in Poland is much smaller, being reduced by a number of large projects undertaken by companies from other countries, and at the turn of 1991 probably came to about 25 per cent. The recent arrival on the Polish market of some large German corporations (Siemens, for example) will eventually increase the role of this country.

In Czechoslovakia, Romania, and Bulgaria where the total number of foreign enterprises is still on the small side and only a few German firms are involved, they nevertheless also play a very significant role. German capital is financing the biggest investment project currently under way in Czechoslovakia: expansion of the Skoda auto-manufacturing enterprise which is now part-owned by Volkswagen.

Germany's biggest competitors in Eastern Europe are Italy, Austria, France, and the USA. Enterprises from other countries have so far been less active. A particularly vigorous drive has been launched by Italian companies. We described in an earlier chapter the wide-ranging operations of Fiat which is seeking technological domination of the expanding car markets of Poland and Yugoslavia. Investment in Eastern Europe has also been undertaken by hundreds of other producers, mostly in the form of joint ventures.

In Yugoslavia the share of Italian enterprises in all foreign investment grew from 12.5 per cent in 1968–88 to 17.5 per cent in 1989.[3] Most of the funds came from medium-size firms. An advantage possessed by Italians is the financial backing of their government, especially when a project can be expected to further Italian exports. The chief areas of interest are the Balkan countries and Poland; Hungary and Czechoslovakia have featured less prominently.

British investment is supported by the active policy of the UK government which produces substantial returns on small outlays. A field in which this policy is particularly rewarding is scientific and technical assistance.

Costing little compared to the credits provided for growth purposes by other countries, it has resulted in training being provided in the United Kingdom or by British-funded schemes in Eastern Europe for a large number of persons with crucial roles to play in economic life, such as senior officials (including ministers and heads of government agencies), managers and co-owners of enterprises, and researchers. The help received in other such areas – for instance, courses for future stockbrokers organized in the City – will also be of long-range benefit and facilitate investment activities.

Prior to 1990 British companies were very wary of investing in Eastern Europe. Their commitment was small: in Yugoslavia, for instance, where the overall value of foreign investment in 1989 amounted to 339 million dollars, only 6 million came from the United Kingdom. The number of investors was also small: seventeen out of 578 (eight out of 234 in Hungary in 1989). In 1990 there came a substantial upswing in British investment, but it still trails far behind that of the leading competitors. The largest number of enterprises are to be found in Poland (seventy five in mid-1990) and Hungary. Among the biggest projects undertaken by British firms is the expansion of a glass foundry in Sandomierz (Poland) by Pilkington which acquired part-ownership of this enterprise and made possible the 140 million dollar investment required for its development. Among its products will be special float glass which is used for car windows.

What has become almost a British specialty is consultancy. Over a dozen firms from the United Kingdom are now involved in Eastern Europe; some have opened large offices. Also increasingly active are various kinds of promoters selling large development projects such as commercial centres, residential estates, warehouse complexes, and industrial parks. Problems with local officialdom and frequently conflicting regulations have so far prevented most of these theoretically highly profitable schemes from going ahead.

Considerable interest has been aroused in British business circles by the information that it will be possible to acquire shares in privatized state enterprises. Since there is a prospect of considerable capital gains in this sphere, it will undoubtedly be treated as an area of portfolio investment well worth exploring. Investors will be assisted by such new institutions as the corporate finance team formed in London by Bankers Trust Company in April 1991. Special investment funds have also been created in the United Kingdom in order to direct investment to Eastern European markets.

One of the countries among the first to become interested in investment in Eastern Europe was Austria. This was due not only to geography and history, though to an even greater extent than in the case of Germany, but also to the Austrian government's hopes of turning this country into 'a bridge between East and West' (similar ambitions are also entertained by certain East European countries). Austrian investment in Eastern Europe up to the end of 1990 was several times larger than British investment and, contrary to some affirmations, it is mostly effected by enterprises belonging to owners from this country (including some state-controlled enterprises like Voerst). Its scale and significance were greatest in Hungary where at the end of 1989 there were sixty-three Austrian-backed joint ventures which accounted for 21 per cent of the capital stock of all foreign enterprises in that country. By January 1991, the number of Austrian enterprises in Hungary increased to 900. In Poland there were 111 Austrian enterprises registered in mid-1990.

The markets of all the East European countries have also been entered by French enterprises. None too visible prior to 1988, they have since begun to make up ground. In 1989 they accounted for over 12 per cent of all foreign investment in Yugoslavia and 9 per cent in Czechoslovakia. In Poland there were sixty-four French companies in mid-1990. The first significant projects were adopted in 1991, the major one being the takeover by Thomson of the biggest Polish producer of kinescopes and other parts for TV sets. In Hungary in February 1991 the French company Sanofi completed purchase of a 40 per cent stake in a big pharmaceutical company Chinoin.

Among other European countries note should be made of investment by firms from Sweden and Switzerland (including the joint Swedish–Swiss enterprise ABB which in 1990 planned to spend over 300 million dollars). Without a doubt, the very high labour costs in these two countries will make companies consider moving a part of their operations to Eastern Europe. This decision was taken for example by the Swedish company Electrolux, the world's biggest white goods company. It has already obtained some success in Hungary, where in March 1991 it acquired Lehel, Hungary's leading refrigerator company. Another big Swedish company, IKEA, began its East European offensive in 1990 by opening a store in Budapest. Later it signed agreements for cooperation with some East European manufacturers of furniture, waiting for the moment when privatization will permit their takeover.

Investment by enterprises in the remaining countries of Western Europe up to the end of 1990 has been very small, totalling less than 200 million dollars. In such countries as Denmark, Finland, Norway, Belgium, the Netherlands, Iceland and Spain knowledge of investment opportunities in Eastern Europe remained very scant. Trade was at too low a level to act as an inducement to investment.

Among non-European countries over 90 per cent of foreign investment comes from the United States. However, only a few of the big American corporations have decided to embark on large-scale projects (one of them being General Electric). For a large number of American firms securing some kind of foothold in Eastern Europe has become an interesting element in their overseas strategy; but most of them prefer to avoid any major commitment of funds.

There are increasingly frequent reports of medium-size industrial establishments being bought or built by well-known American companies: Ford, for instance, is developing an automobile parts plant in Hungary. Such projects are not only a stepping stone to new markets, but also a way of acquiring experience that can be capitalized on in operations on a larger scale. But it was only in 1990 that there came the first announcements of any such major American ventures.

It should not be forgotten when discussing American investment that the United States is also the source of over half the investments made by persons of East European extraction. Enterprises, both large and small, belonging to businessmen of Polish, Hungarian, or Yugoslav origin have established an active presence in these countries, and their involvement will continue to grow.

Taking Eastern Europe as a whole, the share of American enterprises in foreign investment can be put at about 10 per cent. In mid-1990 it was smaller in Poland (only 102 companies and 5 per cent of capital stock), but much larger in Hungary and Yugoslavia.

Investment from other non-European countries at the turn of 1991 was still next to negligible. Representatives of big Japanese, Korean, and Canadian companies are now visiting Budapest, Warsaw, and Belgrade to explore the possibilities of investment. The most significant breakthrough would probably be penetration by Japanese companies, not only the big industrial corporations, but also the large trading organizations known as sogo sosha which have developed a business model exceptionally well suited to the conditions now obtaining on the East European market. Their activities are not confined solely to the purchase, storage and sale of merchandise; in practice they also tend to become involved on the production side.

The Japanese sogo sosha first became interested in Eastern Europe in 1990. Missions which included representatives of banks and industrial enterprises were sent to these countries and resulted in the first investment projects. Their purpose is expansion of the volume of trade. This is simple enough in the case of Japanese exports; it is much more difficult to find East European products that can and will sell in Japan. Concern with developing profitable import lines is the reason for such moves as the formation by one of the sogo sosha, Marubeni, of a company in Hungary producing apple juice for export to Japan. Another of them is contemplating, among other goals, promotion of Japanese tourism in Eastern Europe. The Japanese methods of expansion are being copied by Korean firms which in 1990 opened numerous offices in Eastern Europe.

COUNTRIES OF DESTINATION

The geographical structure of the destination of foreign investment in Eastern Europe is extremely uneven. Over 80 per cent has so far been shared by three countries: Yugoslavia, Poland, and Hungary. In each of them the value of projects completed or in progress has passed the 2 billion dollar mark and will soon top 3 billion. Meanwhile in all the other countries total investment still falls short of half a billion. This can, of course, be largely attributed to political factors: prior to 1990 the regulations in force in Czechoslovakia, Romania, Bulgaria, and Albania were a powerful deterrent to foreign investors. Subsequent changes in the political system followed by amendments in legislation have already led to an abrupt increase in foreign enterprises' interest in the possibilities of investment.

The process of foreign investment can be broken down into a number of phases of varying importance.

- In phase 1 market studies and surveys are carried out. They usually start in response to changes in laws and regulations; in the case of enterprises from countries whose interest in particular markets has a long history (e.g. Germany, Austria, Italy) this phase is of short duration, but much longer in the case of enterprises from such countries as Spain, Norway, Belgium, the Netherlands, or Japan.
- Phase 2 consists mainly of exploratory investment in projects on a small scale which enable foreign enterprises to take the temperature of a particular market; this phase may be of very long duration if investors are, on the one hand, interested in the possibilities but, on the other, fear developments in the political situation or decide that the existing regulations (taxation, for instance) are unsatisfactory, but will probably be changed eventually.
- During phase 3 the initiation of larger projects begins. This phase starts when companies conclude that the situation in a particular country is healthy; the first big investors usually benefit from certain particularly favourable circumstances (for instance, very low subscription prices for shares in newly privatized state enterprises), but often still find themselves running into various obstacles and difficulties arising out of a still incompletely reformed legal system, the regulations (or lack of them) governing the functioning of the public administration, etc.
- During phase 4 mass inflow of foreign investment occurs.

While Yugoslavia, Poland, and Hungary are on the threshold of the fourth of these phases, Albania has barely entered the first, and Czechoslovakia, Romania, and Bulgaria are still in the second. However, Czechoslovakia can be expected to pass swiftly into the third and soon join the East European front-runners.

Yugoslavia

As in other East European countries changes in the regulations relating to foreign investment had a direct influence on the number of newly registered enterprises. In 1975–85 a total of 128 enterprises with foreign capital stakes were registered. Following the very relative liberalization of regulations in 1985, a further 117 were launched in 1985–8. The next round of amendments in legislation (in 1988) led to 578 being started in 1989.[4] and 2,091 in the first ten months of 1990. Simultaneously, there was a rise in the financial commitments of investors: to the end of 1987 total foreign investment in Yugoslavia was estimated at 250 million dollars (as against over 800 million in funds contracted).[5] In 1989 alone the volume of investment was put at 340 million dollars and in 1990 topped 1,200 million. The proportions between these figures would look a little different if it were possible to appraise the host of small sums invested by Yugoslav emigrants.

The regulations in the fields of taxation, labour relations, etc. are so complex that many foreign investors still prefer to operate within the framework of contractual joint ventures, though their role in foreign investment as a whole is declining. The number of foreign enterprises starting their own wholly owned branches continues to be small (see Table 6.1).

In terms of geography, foreign investment in Yugoslavia is concentrating to an increasing extent in Slovenia. This republic attracted 28per cent of aggregate investment in Yugoslavia in 1989 and 32 per cent in 1990, while the role of Serbia, which in 1989 still accounted for 34 per cent, is tailing off slightly. It seems likely that in due course an increasingly large share of foreign investment will be attracted by Croatia on account of its favourable location, relatively well-trained human resources, and fairly efficient local government.

Until mid-1991 Yugoslavia occupied first place in Eastern Europe as regards both the number of foreign enterprises and the amount of funds invested. The breaking up of Yugoslavia in 1991 and the devastating war between Serbs and Croats have recently been leading potential investors to back off from the area and turn their attention to other East European countries, primarily Poland, Hungary, and Czechoslovakia.

Table 6.1 Structure of foreign investments in Yugoslavia in 1989 and on 30 September 1990 according to legal forms

Form of foreign investment	Number		Value ($m)		Structure in 1990 (%)
	1989	1990	1989	1990	
Equity joint ventures	390	1,435	146	363	41.5
Contractual joint ventures	92	270	175	429	49.0
Wholly foreign-owned companies	96	286	19	88	9.5
Total	578	1,991	340	880	100.0

Sources: Investing in Yugoslavia, Ljubljana, CICD, 1990, p. 12; M. Rojec, 'Inostrane direktne investicije u YU', *Europa 92*, 1990, No.12, p. 9.

Poland

Until 1986 foreign investment in Poland was statutorily restricted to small business (in reality this notion is not clearly defined by the Polish law). In 1988 there were about 700 firms in this category (see Table 6.2). None of them undertook any major initial investment. The profits earned were high enough to enable a number of them to expand within a few years into medium-sized establishments and some into large manufacturing enterprises. In 1986 there were already 175 'small businesses' employing over 100 persons, including four with over 500.

In 1986 joint ventures appeared on the scene, at first in the form of combinations between Polish state enterprises and foreign investors, but shortly afterwards joined by the first companies wholly owned by the latter. At the end of 1988 a total of only thirty-one joint ventures had been registered, of which twenty were reported to employ over 100 persons (among them, one with over 1,000). Subsequently, the number of foreign

Table 6.2 Number of foreign-owned small businesses in Poland

	1977–9	*1980–1*	*1982–4*	1985–7	*1988*
Number started	26	87	553	140	67
Number closed	–	5	39	101	25

Sources: J. Kwiatkowski, 'Zagraniczne inwestycje bezposrednie w krajach Europy Wschodniej', *Sprawy Miedzynarodowe*, 1990, No.1, pp. 88–9.

enterprises rose quickly, though it is hard to say how quickly, one reason being that some of the old 'small businesses' re-registered as joint venture companies. By the end of 1990 the Foreign Investment Agency had received close on 3,000 applications for licences to form joint venture companies and of these 2,466 had been approved.[6]

To an increasing extent foreign investors are seeking control of the enterprises of which they are part-owners. Of the 1,538 joint ventures registered in mid-1990 there were only 267 in which their share of the equity was less than 50 per cent; in 244 cases it amounted to 55 per cent and in 545 to over 80 (including some that were wholly owned).[7] The amount of capital put up by foreign investors tended to be small, exceeding 1 million dollars only in twenty-six cases. In practice it is impossible to estimate the total amount of capital expenditure to date.

To the end of 1989 there were no single large-scale projects undertaken by foreign enterprises. In 1990 a number of deals of this kind were concluded, the most important involving Asea Brown Boveri (which plans to invest over ٪٠٠ million dollars in production of electrical machinery, turbines, etc.). Substantial investments are to be undertaken by Siemens of Germany (production of telephone exchanges), Chase Enterprise of the USA (cable television), Pilkington of the United Kingdom (float glass), Intercell of Sweden, Coca Cola of the USA, Hyatt Regency Warsaw of the Netherlands, MacKenzie Methane of the USA (methane extraction), Philips of the Netherlands (electric bulbs).

Table 6.3 Regional distribution of joint venture companies in Poland on 30 June 1990

Voivodship	Number of companies	Value of initial capital (thousands of dollars)
Warsaw	453	97,721
Gdansk	88	64,504
Szczecin	113	54,504
Poznan	127	15,246
Katowice	98	14,035
Zielona Gora	33	12,421
Olsztyn	23	10,551
Others	603	173,906
Total	1,538	442,888

Source: E. Sadowska-Cieslik, *Analysis of Licensces Granted by Foreign Investment Companies*, Warsaw, Foreign Investment Agency, 1990, mimeo, Table 6.

As regards geography, companies with a foreign capital stake are most numerous in the voivodships (provinces) of Warsaw, Poznan, and Szczecin. Although the geographical structure of investment cannot be mapped accurately, the size of the capital stock of companies is on record. In mid-1990 it was largest in the Warsaw, Gdansk, and Szczecin voivodships. This suggests a tendency on the part of foreign investors to be drawn chiefly to the country's capital and principal ports (see Table 6.3).

The geographical structure of foreign investment in Poland is largely fortuitous. As in other East European countries, no attempt has been made to use foreign investment as a means of stimulating growth in the most underdeveloped regions by offering tax reliefs and other incentives. Given these areas' inferior infrastructure, their usually less efficient local governments, higher transport costs, etc., the absence of such a policy will make for a concentration of investment in a few privileged locations.

Hungary

The first four Hungarian joint ventures with foreign capital stakes were set up before 1980. At the end of 1980 there were thirty two and 107 in October 1987.[8] In 1988 the number of registered foreign enterprises grew to 288 and in January 1991 to 3,900 (see Table 6.4). About 50 per cent of them are commercial firms; manufacturing enterprises numbered were 800.[9] The

Table 6.4 Top foreign investments in Hungary

Investor	Nationality	Share (%)	Deal (£m)	Joint venture and sector
Sanofi	French	40	75	Chinoin – pharmaceuticals
General Electric	American	50	150	GE Tungsram – lighting
Guardian Glass	American	80	115	Hunguard – glass
Ford	American	100	83	Ford Hungaria – vehicles
Prinahorn Group	Austrian	40	82	Dunapack – paper
General Motors	American	67	66	GM Hungary – vehicles
Electrolux	Swedish	100	65	Lehel – refrigerators
Sara Lee	American	51	60	Compack – food
Nestlé	Swiss	97	38	Nestlé Intercsocolade – food
Agrana	Austrian	49	35	Szabadegyhazi Szeszipari – food
Suzuki	Japanese	40	30	Magyar Suzuki – vehicles

Source: N. Denton, 'Hungary takes the lead on foreign investment', *Financial Times*, 1991, 14 May, p. 2.

capital stock of these enterprises was estimated in October 1990 to be in the region of 750 million dollars. Foreign companies' and joint ventures' financial reports showed 1,810 million dollars of accumulated foreign investment at September 1991, compared to 1,530 million dollars at the end of 1990. A large proportion of foreign investment is realized through joint ventures which have taken over one-time state-owned factories and embarked on intensive modernization of production. In many of them the structure of production is being radically overhauled which often involves its reorientation (for instance, some establishments which directed their products to the Soviet Union and Eastern Europe are now marketing a growing proportion of their new range in the West).

Hungary is also the East European country which has attracted the greatest foreign indirect investment though in its circumstances it is hard to draw a line between direct and indirect in many cases. In fact investors with minority holdings do not seem to have reached as yet any strategic decisions.

Czechoslovakia

The first large joint ventures were started in Czechoslovakia in the mid-1980s. The new regulations issued in 1988 encouraged several dozen foreign firms to invest on a small scale. On 1 October 1989 there were twenty-four joint ventures registered in Czechoslovakia, all of them small.

Their equity value was estimated at 55 million dollars. Although no legal limitations were placed on the size of foreign capital stakes, there was no joint venture in which it exceeded 50 per cent. At the turn of 1991 no big or even medium project involving foreign funds had yet been undertaken in Czechoslovakia, unless we include the construction of a number of hotels by foreign contractors.

The attitude of foreign enterprises to Czechoslovakia altered radically as a result of the political changes in late 1989. In 1990 large numbers of representatives of leading companies paid fact-finding visits, pending the introduction of more liberal foreign investment regulations and the commencement of privatization processes (which duly came about at the beginning of 1991).

A number of corporations began negotiations with the Czechoslovak government with a view to buying into certain specified enterprises on special terms. One such company was Bata, wanting to repossess its original factories. Others are Volkswagen, which is now taking over Skoda, General Motors, and Siemens. Many Western enterprises, anticipating new regulations, set up small companies to gain the necessary experience. In November 1990 there were 420 joint ventures registered in Czechoslovakia. By October 1991 the number had increased to some 3,040.

Most of them are very small enterprises, some belonging to large Western companies which wish to be present on this new market. At the end of 1991 the majority had not yet been in business long enough to invest on any significant scale. Czechoslovakian authorities believe that foreign investment in this country will now grow rapidly.

Romania

A policy aimed at attracting foreign capital was put into operation in Romania as early as the beginning of the 1970s. The 1971 regulations, which legalized foreign investment, aroused considerable interest in the Western business world (especially in France and Italy) and Bucharest was visited by many representatives of foreign companies. However, almost all of them came to the conclusion that any decision to go ahead with investment would be premature. Nevertheless, in the course of the 1970s nine joint ventures were started with foreign equity capital participation. The investment expenditure of these companies was not, however, significant; moreover in the next decade their number dwindled (to seven in 1980 and five in 1987).

A certain revival of interest in Romania was sparked by the overthrow of the Ceaucescu dictatorship in 1990. However, Romania's very difficult economic situation, persistent and acute political strife, and inconsistencies in government policy towards investors made them hesitant to commit themselves.

Negotiations are in progress with a number of firms including a French company which is expected to carry out the modernization of four sugar factories, another French company which is interested in building an 80 million dollar trade centre, and a German company which is thinking of chocolate manufacture and coffee conditioning. By mid-1991 the total number of joint ventures was 4,196, but the value of registered foreign capital was only 192 million dollars.

Bulgaria

The first joint ventures with foreign capital stakes – eight in all – were launched in Bulgaria in 1980. Prior to the introduction in 1989 of new regulations relating to the operation of foreign enterprises their number grew only slightly (in 1987, for instance, there were no more than ten) and the volume of investment actually carried out to the end of 1990 fell well short of 20 million dollars. The 1989 regulations encouraged another dozen or so foreign enterprises to enter into joint ventures, but essentially the atmosphere remained one of wait-and-see. The basic reason why foreign enterprises have not proceeded with investment projects seems to have been that they preferred to bide their time pending a definitive end of communist rule.

Albania

Until mid-1990 a constitutional ban on the ownership of means of production and property in Albania by foreign nationals prevented any foreign investment in this country. The changes in economic policy made by the Albanian leaders in 1990 plus democratization and alterations in the regulations governing foreign enterprise aroused a certain degree of interest on the part, for instance, of firms involved in tourism. In the future attention could also focus on Albania's mineral resources. In January 1991 the first bank with a foreign capital holding was opened primarily for the purpose of handling the finances of foreign enterprises.

To sum up, 80 per cent of foreign investment in Eastern Europe to date has come from Western Europe (chiefly Germany, Austria, Italy, France, Sweden, Switzerland, and the United Kingdom) and 10 per cent from the United States. About 90 per cent of the funds committed to the end of 1990 has gone to three countries – Yugoslavia, Hungary, and Poland – and only about 10 per cent to the remaining four: Czechoslovakia, Romania, Bulgaria, and Albania. Both the scale and geographical structure of foreign investment are now changing very swiftly, largely due to rapidly growing involvement in Czechoslovakia. It seems likely that in the immediate future we will be looking at two clearly distinct areas: north, encompassing Poland, Hungary, Czechoslovakia, and northern Yugoslavia, and South, comprising the remaining nations. The northern part will continue to attract the major portion (probably over 75 per cent) of foreign investment, despite positive changes in the southern half.

FREE TRADE AREAS

In the foregoing sections we discussed investment undertaken in what are normal parts of the national territory of the seven East European countries. However, it is worth saying something about investment of a different type, that is directed towards free trade areas exempt from customs duties and many other regulations of the countries in which they are located. Without a doubt, lack of stability in the rules governing foreign enterprises increases investors' interest in such free trade areas. Here they expect to enjoy the security of operating in a stable environment insulated from changes in regulations affecting the rest of a country.

Foreign trade zones have a very long history in the world at large, during which they have undergone significant transformations. In the last two decades they have been multiplying swiftly and tending towards specialization. Particularly rapid has been the growth the number in which the principal activity is manufacturing. Usually called either duty-free export-processing zones or export-processing free zones, they are subject to specific tax regulations and in many cases exempt from labour relations laws. Even when taxes are the same as in the rest of the country there are many advantages to investment in these enclaves, the most frequent being:

• greater stability of regulations;
• minimalization of bureaucratic barriers, irksome inspections, etc.;
• exemption from labour relations laws, including those relating to dismissal of employees;
• absence of restrictions on profit transfers, bank remittances, etc.

The governments of countries which form export-processing free zones treat them as an additional source of hard currency earnings since almost all of the goods produced there are exported abroad (if moved for sale in the adjacent territory they become subject to duty and other charges). In some countries (e.g. Mexico, Malta, Mauritius) such zones are also an important boost to employment.[10]

In Eastern Europe free trade areas are being created in Poland, Hungary, Yugoslavia, and Bulgaria. In Poland where plans for such areas were first drafted in 1988 the basic regulations are: the Council of Ministers ordonnance of 8 July 1988 on movement of goods between foreign trade zones and adjacent territory, two Council of Ministers decrees of 2 June 1989 setting up the first foreign trade zones, and the Tariff Act of 28 December 1989 which regulated in detail the functioning of these zones. Fifteen have been designated, some of which (in Szczecin, Kedzierzyn-Kozle, and Terespol, among others) are already in operation. However, many crucial aspects of these zones (for instance, the powers of their administrative boards) have not yet been settled. It has until now discouraged investment on any larger scale.

In Hungary free trade areas were referred to in a section of the 1988 legislation on foreign investment[11] and some of the regulations relating to customs duty. Among other things, currency (except for forints) may be freely disposed of. As in Poland, enterprises in these free zones have not yet ventured beyond minor financial and commercial operations.

In Yugoslavia the first export-processing free zone was established in January 1987 in the river port in Belgrade and subsequently extended to the adjacent localities of Pancevo and Smerdevo. It operates under the Law on Free Trade and Customs Zones passed in 1990.[12] To enterprises in such zones this extends certain additional privileges which include a three-year tax holiday. At the end of 1991 the zone in question was still a site of preparatory work (such as foundation laying) for the first major investment projects.

In Bulgaria regulations on the establishment and operation of free trade areas were adopted as early as 1987.[13] Article 13 of the Decree on Free Trade Zones included the provision that 'the profit from productive, trading and other economic activity in the zone is exempted from taxes',[14] but taxed at a rate of 30 per cent if goods from the zone were sold in Bulgarian customs territory. These rules were amended by the 1989 Decree on Economic Activity[15] limiting tax holidays to five years after which a tax of 20 per cent is levied on profits. Bulgaria plans to create three free zones, two in river ports on the Danube (Vidyn and Ruse) and the other in the seaport of Burgas.

In Romania free trade zones were contemplated as early as the 1970s, and regulations were duly issued for the establishment of such a zone in the Danube Delta. However, this project never came to fruition.

To sum up, the majority of East European countries intend to create export-processing free zones. Regulations governing their operation have been elaborated, but these are still incomplete. In no country do they envisage the waiving of curtailment of labour relations laws or broader autonomy for the future boards of these free trade areas. Also, most bureaucratic barriers remain in place. Because of this, foreign companies, though interested in such zones, are refraining from investment. If the requisite regulations are quickly issued free trade areas in Eastern Europe could become magnets for certain types of foreign investment, for instance in the production of parts and components for machinery, equipment, cars, etc. destined for foreign factories. This will also have a certain influence on the geographical structure of foreign investment within particular countries.

7   Portfolio investment

COMMON FEATURES OF PORTFOLIO INVESTMENT IN EASTERN EUROPE

Until 1989 the whole foreign-owned property sector in Eastern Europe stemmed from direct investment. Although the law in most of its countries did not explicitly forbid the purchase of small blocks of securities, there was effectively no way in which this could be done. Joint stock companies were few in number and the majority were either wholly or over 99 per cent owned by the state (there were cases in which a charmed circle of private persons was assigned three shares each, with the state controlling the remainder). Normal security trading was out of the question; no East European country had a proper stock exchange.

However, East European governments did contemplate the possibility of attracting another form of portfolio investment: issues of bonds in convertible currencies. The first such plans were drawn up as early as the 1970s and feelers put out to Western banks (mainly Swiss). However, the countries most interested in bond issues – Poland, Hungary, Yugoslavia, and Romania – were heavily indebted and any larger issue was liable to end in fiasco. In the 1980s indebtedness grew even greater (in some cases by 100 per cent and more), which further reduced the chances of government bond issues in foreign financial markets. Bonds sold on internal markets had no foreign purchasers.

The situation improved slightly in 1991. An improvement in some East European countries' balance of trade and debt rescheduling agreements produced conditions in which bond issues could again be considered. Hungary issued bonds for DM200 million in March 1991 and announced that 1 billion dollars' worth of bonds would be issued until the end of 1991. The prospects of government securities of other countries are still uncertain, but some large privatized enterprises known in the West seem to have much more chances to succeed in issuing their own bonds. There can be no doubt that such issues will begin within a matter of months and that the rate of interest will be higher than that available in the West European securities markets.

Bond purchases will, however, comprise only a small proportion of the portfolio investments of foreign enterprises in Eastern Europe. The basic form will be share purchases. This is directly connected with the acceleration of privatization processes. In a majority of East European countries between mid-1990 and the end of 1993 enterprises accounting for over half of the national product will pass out of state control. This operation, whose scale has no precedent anywhere in the world, will be carried out with the active participation of foreign investors who are being offered a rapidly growing number of shares in privatized enterprises.

The first sell-offs of state-owned enterprises in which foreign capital was involved were carried out under the terms of agreements concluded with certain selected companies. Foreign firms were thus able to acquire large share holdings in privatized enterprises which gave them an effective say in management or even in some cases control. The first portfolio investments of substantial dimensions came with the partial privatization of the Hungarian tourist enterprise Ibusz in which shares were bought by many thousands of small investors. In June 1990 some 40 per cent of the shares were sold, over half (330,000 out of 480,000) on Western exchanges.

As a result of a good promotion campaign, the market value of the stock in Vienna, for instance, climbed in a matter of days from an opening price of 893 schillings to 2,000.[1] In Poland shares in the Universal foreign trade enterprise were put out to public subscription between 7 May and 6 August 1990. Of the 9,846,000 shares on sale just over half (5 million) were offered to foreign investors. They were bought by 102 different purchasers.[2] Although the valuation of the enterprises sold off was very controversial, the fact remains that demand exceeded supply. This encouraged the governments of Hungary and Poland, and subsequently other countries as well, to embark on a rapid expansion of the range of share issues offered to foreign subscribers.

Simplifying a little, we can say we are looking to at least two types of sales of shares to foreign investors: 'spontaneous' and 'statutory'. The first type occurs most frequently when a sell-off decision is taken under the terms of a special agreement concluded with one or more designated foreign buyers. If the enterprises in question are state owned, the right to decide to draw up the specific procedure for sales of shares is in all the East European countries vested by law in the Council of Ministers plus, in some cases, certain special institutions (such as a privatization agency). 'Spontaneous' privatization under which a percentage of shares are sold to foreign investors is of particular significance in sectors of the economy rated of crucial importance, which includes key enterprises in the engineering industry, production of automobiles and other means of transportation, communications, and radio and television. In such 'spontaneous' privatization typical portfolio investment has so far played a minor role, the majority of buyers being large Western companies interested in ownership or part-ownership of privatized enterprises over a longer time period.

A different situation usually arises in the case of 'statutory' privatization. This simply refers to the type of privatization carried out according to the principles specifically laid down in the legislation on privatization of state-owned enterprises successively enacted in the East European countries. The rules relating to the sale of shares in privatized enterprises vary in each of them, partly because of their differing political and economic circumstances. However, they have certain features in common:

- appointment of a specific institution (e.g. privatization agency, ministry of ownership changes, or the like) to monitor and oversee the privatization process on behalf of the government, the heads of these bodies being given considerable powers;
- reservation of the right of the government to make exceptions to the rules;
- allocation of a specified quantity of shares for free distribution or sale at a nominal price to the general public (in the form of vouchers convertible into shares);
- restriction of foreign nationals and enterprises to a certain percentage of shares.

This last provision may simply spring from the fact that a significant part of the issue is reserved for other purposes (e.g. sale at a discount to the work-forces of privatized enterprises). Restrictions may also assume a more specific form – for instance, prohibition of the acquisition of more than 20 per cent of an issue by a single foreign buyer, which means that in such cases foreign investment is solely of a portfolio nature. Obviously, a large proportion of the shares acquired by domestic buyers (individuals or institutions) will be rapidly resold and no doubt many of the persons who obtain vouchers will also wish to trade them. Where possible this will be done on stock exchanges, which will give foreign investors an opportunity to augment their holdings.

The basic purpose of most portfolio investment is the purchase and sale of securities at a profit (sometimes after a considerable lapse of time). Since new investment opportunities arouse the interest of a wide circle of potential purchasers, recent months have seen a stream of articles on this subject in the Western press, many of them based on assessments by specialized firms. One of their features are projections of the expected capital gains. These are speculations without any substance in fact. All that is certain is the subscription price of shares in East European enterprises; nothing, however, can be said about the probable market value of the majority of these shares. There are still no rational mechanisms for investment appraisal.

In the next few months only a few East European enterprises are likely to start being quoted on Western exchanges. The business done on the exchanges already operating in Eastern Europe is still very small, and the price movements largely haphazard. So, too, are the prices at which shares are sold in private transactions not carried out through brokers. For this reason any estimates of the profitability of investments in Eastern Europe are in practice questionable. Because of the balance between the high degree of risk and the potentially large gains, the most advantageous policy for small and medium investors would seem to be the purchase of limited quantities of shares and holding them until there are properly functioning securities exchanges in Eastern Europe. That is also the advice of Tyndall Holdings Plc., which recommends limiting East European securities to no more than 10 per cent of a private investor's portfolio.[3] Some of these investments are made through specialized funds; one such is The Emerging Eastern Europe Fund Ltd (Table 7.1). Many large banks, acting largely as intermediaries, are also showing interest in portfolio investment in Eastern Europe, looking no doubt not only to expansion of their range of operations but also prospective profits.

HUNGARY

The first East European country to embark on efforts to attract foreign portfolio investment was Hungary. The passage of the Company Act in 1989 opened the way to the issue and trading of shares, which gave rise to a securities market almost immediately. As a result of the transformation of some industrial and wholesale companies the shares of some thirty relatively large enterprises gained access to informal stock exchange trading. In January 1990 the Public Issue and Trading Act created a legal, regulatory, and supervisory framework for a securities market.[4] It laid down rules for investors by specifying the requirements for the public offering and trading of bonds and shares which include proper disclosure procedures and prohibition of insider trading. Share issues will be monitored by a public Supervisory Agency. The legal framework was thus created for the establishment of a recognized securities exchange. This made possible the opening on 21 June 1990 of the Budapest Stock Exchange (which had been closed in 1948). It was the first real stock exchange to be opened in a Warsaw Pact country (in both Hungary and Poland certain institutions also called stock exchanges had been operating much earlier, but on lines which effectively resembled ordinary auctions).

Hungary, therefore, rapidly developed machinery facilitating foreign portfolio investment. At first, however, there was little to trade. Spontaneous privatization ran into sharp criticism in Hungary and the government decided to control the process. A State Property Agency was set up to supervise privatization and in September 1990 it published a 'First Privatization Programme'. Under this programme (soon modified) there began at the end of 1990 the privatization of a large number of well-run and profitable state enterprises, chiefly in the chemical, pharmaceutical, and engineering industries and in distribution and tourism. The privatization operation can be divided into a number of phases:

1 selection of enterprises and negotiation of the terms of privatization (with management and work-force representatives);
2 valuation of these enterprises carried out by firms selected in an open tender which are able to provide comprehensive corporate finance (very often, international investment banks);
3 public offering of shares sold according to the agreed principles;
4 election of enterprises' governing bodies by the new shareholders.

Table 7.1 Selected Eastern Europe's specialized funds

Fund	Sponsors	Size (m)	Targets
Eastern Europe Development Fund	Invesco MIM Dawa Europe	$40	Export oriented
Austro-Hungary Fund	Merrill Lynch	$45.5	Austrian and Hungarian listed stocks
Hungarian Inv't Co.	Kleinwort Benson	$100	Export, tourism, trading
First Hungary Fund	Bank of Hungary, Andrew Sartos	$80	Service sectors, privatization operations
Emerging Eastern Europe Fund	Georges Soros, Bear, Stearns and Co.	$15	Dept equity swaps export oriented
Deutschland Investments Corporation	Robert Fleming	DM96	Construction, retail, service sectors
Central and East European Partnership	Robert Maxwell	$250	Publishing, property, construction
Creditanstalt Hungary Fund	Creditanstalt Bankveren	$50	Hungarian listed stocks

Source: S. Antunes, 'In East Europe, a push for Privatization', *Financial Times*, 1991, 25 May, p. 15.

The practical issues of the process of privatization vary slightly in different cases. The most usual procedure is to reserve a percentage of the share issue for foreign investors, but its size depends on the sector of the economy and the expected demand on the part of Hungarian investors. In practice the amount of equity in the enterprises designated by the First Privatization Programme that can be acquired by foreign investors ranges from 10 to 40 per cent. In some cases part of the issue is reserved for professional investors in order to strengthen their position in an otherwise very competitive market.[5]

Another strategy has been adopted for lame-duck enterprises. In Hungary as in other East European countries this is a category which is very large and in recent months has become larger still as a result of such factors, among others, as declining exports to the Soviet Union and the other countries of the region in question. Such enterprises require injections not only of capital but also of new technologies, reorganization, and cuts in work-forces. In this respect the Hungarian government is pinning particularly great hopes on foreign investors. 'These enterprises cannot think of public offering; even if they are able to raise secondary funds from portfolio investors, the latter can only be selected by a private placement.'[6] Consequently, joint ventures are being created to which the Hungarian partner contributes 'the healthy hard core of these bankrupt enterprises as an in-kind contribution', while the new investors' input comprises finance, machinery, licences, etc. These new investors are on the whole (and sometimes solely) foreign businessmen and enterprises. Some of them treat buying into a company as typically direct investment, but a growing number see it as portfolio investment. Once a company has been put back on its feet the value of its stock rises swiftly and the returns on the investment are likely to be very large. The sale of the shares will then produce a very satisfactory capital gain. On the other hand, there can be no question that there is considerable risk involved – for the usual technical reasons whenever a part of an enterprise is bought, and also on account of the difficulties that may arise in laying off personnel (which is often a prerequisite of the profitability of a venture).

All in all, therefore, foreign investors are offered a choice in Hungary between a growing number of enterprises sold off in a variety of ways. While it is likely that average subscription prices will remain low, there will undoubtedly be considerable risk attached to the purchase of shares in particular enterprises. Consequently, it will become an increasingly frequent practice to acquire portfolios composed of shares in a number of different enterprises.

Portfolio investment will be facilitated by the existence of a securities exchange. It must, however, be realized that it will be a long time before the

Budapest Stock Exchange can be compared with its large counterparts in the West. For the first months it was housed in a small room on the first floor of the International Trade Centre and was open for trading for no more than one hour per day (and three days a week). In late 1990 it moved into a bigger, but still a single, room and introduced longer hours of business; but it still has a long way to go. Nevertheless, the existence of the Budapest Stock Exchange has made it possible to put some Hungarian securities on Western markets where they are purchased by cautious investors. The biggest role in this respect is played by the Vienna Stock Exchange. In due course the significance of the Budapest Stock Exchange will grow.

The first year of the Budapest Stock Exchange disappointed foreign investors because of an error made by its promoters. Its start was too good: the price of shares offered to the public increased too much. It generated a subsequent fall in the prices of shares, for example shares in Ibusz dropped from 2,000 to 700 shillings. Hungarian and Austrian stock exchange experts, however, are remaining optimistic, being sure that shares' quotations will now begin to go up again and the volume of transactions on Hungarian titles will increase quickly.

YUGOSLAVIA

The privatization process, begun in Yugoslavia on a small scale in 1990 and speeded up in 1991, ushered in the first portfolio investment. From the regulations issued it can be concluded that the central government views the sale to foreigners of shares in privatized enterprises as 'a lesser evil', that is as an expedient enabling stock to be disposed of in a situation in which the demand among Yugoslav nationals is small. The 1990 regulations[7] divide purchasers of shares in privatized enterprises into two categories: employees of the enterprises concerned and others. In sales to employees, valuation is made on the basis of the balance sheet for the previous year; in the case of other buyers the criterion is market value.

Needless to say, foreign investors belong to the latter category. The Yugoslav legislation has been supplemented by regulations issued in each republic, and these increase the unequal treatment of different purchasers. For example, in Slovenia the 1990 Privatization of Companies Act requires foreign purchasers to pay at least 60 per cent of the price of the shares in cash while for other buyers this mark is set at 30 per cent.[8]

The privatization process in each of the republics is overseen by their own supervisory bodies (e.g. the Agency for Privatization of the Republic of Slovenia) which lay down the rules for share issues. One is the selection of purchasers through auctions. On the other hand, there are no restrictions on the quantity of shares in privatized enterprises that may be bought.

Despite the unequal treatment of purchasers, foreign investors can count on relatively low share prices (by comparison with the actual worth of the enterprises concerned). The scale of their commitment will to a large extent depend on the evolution of the political situation in Yugoslavia.

In December 1989 two exchanges were opened in Yugoslavia which have facilitated portfolio investment. On 26 December a small but go-ahead Yugoslav Stock Exchange went into operation in Ljubljana and a day later the Yugoslav Capital Market in Belgrade. In March 1990 they were joined by a third in the capital of Croatia, Zagreb. All three are the property of Yugoslav banks and other financial institutions. The volume of trading on these exchanges has so far been very small, which has resulted in hours of business being short. The Yugoslav Capital Market, for instance, holds only one brief session a week and had an estimated turnover in 1990 of only about a million dollars. That of the Ljubljana exchange came to 10 million dollars in 1990. The prospects of these stock exchanges mainly depend on the supply of Yugoslav companies willing to have their securities quoted.[9]

POLAND

Spontaneous privatization of several dozen enterprises in Poland has en-abled a small number of foreign buyers to purchase shares in the stock of some of them.

In July 1990 a privatization law was enacted which includes provisions relating to share purchases by foreigners.[10] In practice many specific and crucial aspects of privatization are regulated by the Ministry of Ownership Changes which has broad powers. In theory, foreign investors may buy up to 80 per cent of the stock of privatized enterprises (20 per cent being set aside for sale at a discount to their work-forces). The reality, however, has been that in particular cases a smaller percentage of shares has been offered and the ceiling on the quantity that can be purchased by foreign buyers kept below 30 per cent. For example, bids were invited from Western investors for 17.5 per cent of the shares in a big construction company, Exbud, sold off in December 1990, and for 20 per cent in Prosper Bank SA.

The actual prices paid for shares by foreign investors in 1990 were very low. To prevent foreigners from acquiring controlling interests in Polish companies on the cheap the Privatization Act limits the amount of shares that can be bought by a single investor to 10 per cent of the stock. This restriction can be waived on a case-by-case basis by the chairman of the Foreign Investment Agency. In practice, therefore, preference has been given to typically portfolio investment, though the Polish government hopes that foreign shareholders will seek in their own interests to exert some influence on the running of enterprises since it goes without saying that improvements in management will increase the value of their holdings. Article 33 of the Act allows profits from the sale of shares to be remitted abroad after payment of a capital gains tax.

Because of the immense scale on which privatization processes are going ahead in Poland, the blocks of shares offered to foreign investors will total a very great value. Despite relatively low appraisals of the assets of newly privatized enterprises, we will be looking at an issue worth many billions of dollars. The success of the operation will depend to a large extent on improvements in the efficiency of Polish banks and stock exchanges.

As early as the 1970s there were occasional public meetings of buyers and sellers which were called 'stock exchanges'. But it was only in late 1990 that a Public Trading and Securities Act was passed which opens the way to the establishment of a normal modern stock exchange. It will not open until mid-1991 when brokers have returned from training courses abroad and the securities market will be big enough to guarantee a substantial level of business. It is expected that a growing proportion of the trading on the Warsaw exchange will be for the account of foreign investors.

OTHER EAST EUROPEAN COUNTRIES

In the other East European countries portfolio investment has so far been either impossible or very small. This will change as privatization processes gather momentum.

In Czechoslovakia government property is being privatized, but not according to one blanket formula. In each case a blueprint is drawn up by the management of an enterprise and eventually approved following a complex fine-tuning procedure. Enterprises themselves decide what proportion of their stock can be acquired by foreign investors. It is expected that vouchers will be distributed at a nominal price to the whole adult population of Czechoslovakia, for which at least 40 per cent of the share capital of newly privatized enterprises may be purchased (in particular cases this proportion will vary but an upper limit has been set of 80 per cent). The very considerable value of these vouchers means that in practice it will be Czechoslovak citizens who acquire that 80 per cent stake in the stock of the best-known and most prestigious firms among the enterprises to be privatized along the lines mentioned.

Foreign investors will be able to acquire majority holdings in smaller enterprises but with the prospect, once a secondary securities market has developed, of purchasing shares in the big companies from their Czechoslovak owners. Although it is too early to say what actual use will be made of these opportunities, there can be no doubt that portfolio investment in Czechoslovakia is of interest to a number of investment companies in Germany and Austria. It is worth pointing out that some Czechoslovak enterprises will be privatized in completely different ways which will include transformation into joint ventures involving foreign companies.

In Bulgaria and Romania portfolio investment on a wider scale will probably commence in 1992, but it is hard to expect the volume of transactions to take off at once and attain significant dimensions. In Albania the new political situation permits us to draw the same conclusions.

Summing up, we can say that foreign portfolio investment in Eastern Europe has so far been very small. The pioneering role in promoting it is being played by Hungary; in the not too distant future a very marked increase in portfolio investment can be expected in Poland and, in all probability, in Czechoslovaki and Slovenia. The other countries are still at the stage of discussing the possibilities of encouraging this kind of investment.

The experience to date is too scant to allow any firm conclusions to be drawn about the effective influence of portfolio investment on the future performance of privatized enterprises. Optimists hope that foreign investors will in their own interests seek to pave the way to change and introduce new work methods and technologies, areas in which there is much that they can do. Pessimists take the view that they will behave in the traditional manner of portfolio investors and simply wait for change to come about automatically under the impact of market forces, satisfied that this will yield them substantial gains within a reasonable period of time. However, it is beyond question that in Eastern Europe as a whole portfolio investment in the years immediately ahead will be one of the most important factors accelerating the progress of privatization processes. It will also bring these countries hard currency earnings of no mean order.

8 Prospects

The facts presented in the foregoing pages are evidence of a rapid growth of foreign investment in Eastern Europe. It is seen to be a positive economic and political factor by both the investors and the recipient countries. Expansion of foreign private investment is also espoused by Western governments. The West has a stake in the acceleration of systemic change in Eastern Europe and the complete dismantlement of communist structures by the countries of this region. As we have shown, foreign investment acts as a spur to the progress of the privatization process and so is a factor facilitating systemic change. It also expedites modernization of economies, which is of great consequence politically as well as economically.

The West also has a stake in another aspect of foreign investment: its fostering of stronger ties between Eastern Europe and the OECD countries. The result is a growth of mutual trade and fuller participation by the East European countries in the international division of labour.

The favourable attitude of Western governments to private investment in Eastern Europe has important practical consequences, the significance of which will grow in at least three spheres.

1 Promotion of investment. The majority of Western enterprises have a very slender grasp of the realities of East European markets (even if they are persuaded of the contrary) and it is likely, given the region's current personnel and financial situation, that it will be some time before the institutions set up by East European governments to promote foreign investment get fully into their stride. That being so, a large number of the tasks involved will have to be undertaken by Western governments, embassies, and organizations responsible for information and assistance.

2 Guarantees for investors. Unquestionably, there is a great deal of risk attached to direct investment in Eastern Europe, if only because of the frequency with which, as we have seen, legal regulations are changed. Theoretically, investors can insure themselves with private institutions

against every type of risk, but this is an expensive and troublesome business. In these circumstances, particular significance is assumed by diverse forms of government guarantees, some of them built into international agreements concluded between the countries of origin and East European nations. A large number have been signed to date which offer various kinds of investment guarantees, but the process of implementation will be a long one.

3 Credit facilities. The swift growth of the value of foreign investment in Eastern Europe has given banks a greater role to play in this process. As late as 1989 the majority of investment was financed out of enterprises' and entrepreneurs' own funds, supplemented by commercial loans (for machinery purchases, for instance). Since 1990 the situation has changed and it is now long-term bank credits that predominate and will be of growing significance. Because of the huge external debt of the majority of East European countries (see the Appendix, Table A.5), private banks are reluctant to finance such investment, particularly when the applicants are smaller and less well-known Western firms. This makes government guarantees and credits a matter of particular importance.

Naturally, the prospects for foreign investment in Eastern Europe depend not only on the policy of Western governments but also, and to a crucial degree, on internal developments in these countries in three areas: political, economic, and legislative. Optimism about the future of the region, however justified, should not obscure the fact that there are areas in which serious dangers are looming.

In the political field it is beyond question that the dominant trend will be continuing democratization. Some of its consequences may not be appreciated by investors. It is unlikely that many of them will, for instance, view with much favour the organization of unions (hitherto virtually non-existent in foreign enterprises). But, generally speaking, the rapid introduction in Eastern Europe of political and social mechanisms similar to those in the West will be to the long-term advantage of foreign proprietors.

Democratization processes are not, however, guaranteed a smooth passage. Disintegration of the communist system cannot by any means be equated with a total victory for democracy. One of the principal factors in the downfall of communism was the power of national sentiment. In the new situation long-repressed animosities are finding outlets and ethnic issues have suddenly become an acute problem in most of the countries of the region. Only Poland, Hungary, and Albania are relatively homogenous states. Czechoslovakia, however, is a union of two nations and also contains sizeable minorities: Hungarian, Ukrainian, and Polish. Large expanses of central and western Romania are the home of Hungarians (and there are also significant Gypsy and German minorities). In Bulgaria there are many rural districts where a majority of the inhabitants consider themselves Turks. In Yugoslavia there is no majority population group; it is a multi-national state racked by powerful ethnic tensions. This is a situation which could not only trigger off fierce internal conflicts but also generate troubled relations between neighbouring countries. The risks to foreign enterprises are obvious. They fear not only outbreaks of regular fighting, but also a growth of terrorism which is a weapon sometimes resorted to by minorities with no other chance of securing their rights. Consequently, it can be expected that foreign investors will concentrate on politically stable regions and avoid areas inhabited by certain minorities, even though they are ones where new investment is particularly badly needed.

Another threat to foreign investment is the policy of local authorities in poorly developed areas. The example of Yugoslavia seems to indicate that they tend to think chiefly in terms of the present. One of the consequences of such an attitude is the imposition of hefty local taxes (or 'contributions' as they are called in Yugoslavia) on foreign enterprises as a means of raising the money to pay for basic public services and utilities, such as maintenance of schools and hospitals, road construction, etc. Needless to say, this kind of policy drives investors away from such areas.

In the economic field the principal feature of the immediate future will without a doubt be a continuation of systemic change. But the privatization processes that now enjoy almost universal popular support will eventually start to provoke a certain amount of negative social feedback, augmented by the growth of a *nouveau riche* class of not always impeccable back-ground. However, for East European governments there is no alternative to stepping up the pace of privatization, even if the ground has not been fully prepared. The lesson of experience is that the old system is beyond reform, while a realistic 'third way' is something that no one has yet devised. To put it more succinctly: the third way leads to the Third World. Consequently, in every East European country, Bulgaria, Romania, and Albania included, a capitalist system will be quickly put together with all its good and bad features. This, of course, is an environment in which foreign enterprises will feel secure and in their element.

Rapid systemic change will put the East European countries within closer reach of the European Economic Community. In 1990 Hungary, Poland, and Czechoslovakia embarked on negotiations for association with the Community and there can be no doubt that agreements to that effect will be introduced very quickly (probably in 1992). The other countries of the region are also likely to enter into similar negotiations, but in their case they may take longer. Settlement of the association question will give the East European nations substantial tariff privileges on the Community market, which will make a considerable difference to the behaviour of foreign investors (from both Western Europe and overseas). A new factor will arise: investment in Eastern Europe keyed to the West European market. Eventually it will carry even greater weight as the prospect of full membership of the Community materializes.

Admission of the East European countries to the Community has a fair number of supporters. These include, in addition to the believers in a single Europe, business circles in Western Europe interested in expansion eastward. The idea of extending membership to at least some of these countries (Poland, Czechoslovakia, Hungary) will also have the backing of all those who fear dominance of the Community by a reunited Germany. Theoretically, therefore, the outlook for East European entry seems auspicious. However, there are two obstacles:

1 fears in certain quarters that too rapid enlargement of the Community could weaken its cohesion and make it too cumbersome to function efficiently;
2 the EEC machinery whereby aid to backward countries and regions is provided by a variety of common funds (e.g. the European Regional Development Fund).

The latter is the more serious obstacle. In the present situation the Community simply cannot afford the huge expenditures with which it would be faced as a result of the admission of as much as seven new relatively poor members. Consequently, it is likely that there will be increasing support for a novel arrangement of an interim nature: an intermediate status between association and full membership, in other words membership with some but not all the rights. East European countries in this category would not be entitled to grants on normal terms from the agriculture and regional development funds, but this would be offset by smaller financial obligations and the possibility of maintaining certain restrictions on imports from other EEC countries. This would, therefore, be a compromise solution effectively accelerating the adjustment of the economies of the countries concerned to the conditions in the Community. For foreign investors there would be the manifold benefits of the consequent institutional linkages with the Community and the direct gains to be reaped in the sphere of production as a result of easier exports to the West European market. The advantages of the cheapness of labour in Eastern Europe would then manifest themselves in full.

Closer association with the EEC will advance solutions of the acute problem of the East European countries' external debt, especially as over two-thirds of it is owed to Western Europe. Reduction of these liabilities and changes in the terms of payment are now a subject of negotiations. If successful, the governments of at least some of these countries would be more prone to consider the possibility of debt-to-equity swaps. The very low quotation of East European debts on the secondary capital market will increase the attractiveness of such investment, though it might also meet with some resistance in the countries concerned.

As has been frequently emphasized in this book, an indispensable condition for an inflow of foreign investment is the creation of a favourable environment through the introduction of appropriate laws and regulations. It is by no means a foregone conclusion that stabilization of the ground rules will quickly carry the day in all the East European countries. It is a necessity which is not understood by many of the senior civil servants responsible for external economic relations, and this includes the highest echelons of finance ministries. On the other hand, it is certain that in all of these countries major amendments will be made to existing regulations and new legislation passed relating to foreign investment. Also to be expected are reforms of taxation systems which will bring them more into line with those in the EEC (Poland, for instance, is to introduce value-added tax in the course of 1992). This will have a bearing on the taxes payable by foreign enterprises.

Greater difficulties could be posed by the question of guarantees for foreign investors. But this, too, is a problem that will gradually be solved. One of the most important ways in which this can be accomplished is the conclusion of agreements by East European countries containing guarantees insuring foreign enterprises against all risks other than commercial (which, therefore, effectively covers political risk as well). Another type of guarantee would come from membership of the Multilateral Investment Guarantee Agency (MIGA) in which enterprises can be insured for up to 90 per cent of non-commercial losses (to a maximum of 50 million dollars). It seems probable that East European countries will be joining MIGA in the next few years.

The general conclusion is that in the immediate future the situation in the majority of East European countries will continue to evolve in a direction favourable to foreign investors. This will encourage an increasing flow of capital into most of the region. Foreign-owned enterprises will become one of the chief motor forces of economic growth. Thanks to them, the moderni- zation of East European economies and structural change will proceed with even greater momentum. One of the principal results of these changes will be to make Eastern Europe more closely interlocked economically with Western Europe and the world market.

Statistical appendix

Table A.1 Comparative living standards in selected European countries

Country	Cars per 1000	Telephones per 1000	TVs per 1000	Daily calories per capita	Life expectancy
Albania	–	–	83	2713	72
Bulgaria	120	140	191	2855	73
Czechoslovakia	173	240	281	3448	72
Hungary	156	152	402	3569	71
Poland	120	122	263	3336	72
Romania	11	130	166	3373	71
Yugoslavia	131	154	175	3563	73
Ireland	208	265	181	3632	75
Spain	276	396	368	3360	77
United Kingdom	403	524	434	3260	76

Sources: *World Bank Atlas 1990*, Washington, World Bank, 1990, pp. 6–9; *Human Development Report 1991*, UNDP, New York, Oxford University Press, 1991, pp. 119–20, 174, 182.

Table A.2 Employment in per cent of total labour force

Country	Agriculture		Industry	
	1960	*1988*	*1960*	*1988*
Albania	71	54	17	27
Bulgaria	55	20	19	33
Czechoslovakia	24	12	36	37
Hungary	36	18	30	33
Poland	50	28	22	26
Romania	66	29	13	34
Yugoslavia	59	26	23	24

Sources: *World Economic Outlook 1990*, Washington, IMF, 1990, p. 66; *Human Development Report 1991*, op. cit., p. 183.

Table A.3 Production of selected industrial products, 1988

Country	Liquid fuels 000,000 tonnes	Trucks '000	Ships '000 BRT	Synthetics '000 tonnes	Shoes 000,000 pairs
Bulgaria	11.1	9.3	71	319	24.2
Czechoslovakia	12.1	54.2	0	1,152	53.8
Hungary	6.3	13.2	0	539	36.2
Poland	13.2	53.1	139	641	65.6
Romania	20.8	35.4	60	664	53.5
Yugoslavia	–	72.0	479	701	68.7

Source: *Rocznik Statystyczny 1990*, Warsaw, GUS, 1990, pp. 547–64.
Note: The Romanian truck and shoe production figures are for 1981.

Table A.4 Production of selected agricultural products, 1988 (in millions of tonnes)

Country	Cereals	Butter	Sugar	Meat
Bulgaria	7,965	26.6	–	906
Czechoslovakia	11,879	148	660	1,801
Hungary	15,158	35	513	1,740
Poland	26,958	267	1,872	3,172
Romania	31,698	44	430	1,736
Yugoslavia	17,164	–	691	1,588

Source: *Rocznik Statystyczny 1990*, Warsaw, GUS, 1990, pp. 565–73.

Table A.5 External gross debt of Eastern European countries

Country	Total debt (million dollars)		Debt per capita (dollars)
	1970	1989	1989
Bulgaria	700	9,000	1,001
Czechoslovakia	300	5,000	320
Hungary	1,000	20,000	1,947
Poland	1,200	39,900	1,051
Romania	1,000	1,400	60
Yugoslavia	–	21,680	920

Source: ECE Secretariat Common Data Base.
Note: The Romanian debt was totally absorbed in 1990 and the Polish debt was reduced to about 28 billion dollars in March 1991.

Table A.6 East European foreign trade (in millions of dollars)

Country	Export		Import		Balance	
	1980	*1989*	*1980*	*1989*	*1980*	*1989*
Bulgaria	10,372	17,223*	9,650	16,582*	+722	+642*
Czechoslovakia	14,891	14,455	15,148	14,277	−257	+177
Hungary	8,677	9,584	9,235	8,803	−558	+781
Poland	16,997	13,155	19,089	10,085	−2,092	+3,070
Romania	11,401	14,161*	13,201	11,259*	−1,800	+2,902*
Yugoslavia	10,770	13,363	18,279	14,802	−7,509	−1,439
Total	73,108	81,941	84,602	75,808	−11,494	6,133

Source: Monthly Bulletin of Statistics, No. 11, 1990, pp. 96, 98, 110.
Note: *1988.

Notes

1 POLITICAL AND ECONOMIC CHANGE IN EASTERN EUROPE

1 It is worth noting that the geographical centre of Europe is located close to the centre of Poland.
2 A. Kuklinski, 'What Has Happened in Europe in 1989 and 1990?', *Local Development in Europe. Experiences and Prospects*, Warsaw, 1990, University of Warsaw, p. 412.
3 S. Michalowski, *Bezpieczenstwo ekonomiczne w stosunkach Wschod-Zachod*, Warsaw, PISM, 1990, pp. 129–50.
4 G. Mink (ed.), 'Europe de l'Est: la transition', *Problemes politiques et sociaux*, 1990, No.636.
5 *Maly Rocznik Statystyczny 1990*, Warsaw, GUS, 1990, p. 178.
6 Zoltan Roman, *Recent Developments in Privatization in Hungary*, mimeo, October 1990, pp.12–15.
7 'Wkrotce handel calkowicie prywatny', *Zycie Warszawy*, Warsaw, 1990, 17 October, p. 4.
8 *O przebiegu procesow prywatyzacji w strukturze podmiotowej gospodarki w III kwartale tego roku*, Warsaw, CUP, 1990, p. 18.
9 Zoltan Roman, op.cit., pp. 10 and 11.
10 Law on privatization of State-owned enterprises, 1990.
11 Ibid., Chapter 3.
12 'Law no. 15/1990 concerning restructuring of state economic units as self-sufficient administrations and trading companies', *Romanian Economic Digest*, Bucharest, September 1990, pp. 53–70.
13 D. Triska, C. Jelinek-Francis, *A Study of Privatization in the Czech and Slovak Federal Republic*, Prague, mimeo, November 1990, pp. 2–11.
14 See W. Brus, K. Laski, *Von Marx zum Markt. Die sozialistische Lander auf der Suche nach einem neuen Wirtschaftssystem*, Marburg, Metropolis Verlag, 1990.

2 EAST EUROPEAN EXPECTATIONS OF FOREIGN INVESTMENT

1 'Visionary seeks an equal chance', *Financial Times*, 1991, 23 April, p. 23.
2 *Politika*, Belgrade, 1990, 10–16 November, p. 5.

3 R.E. Caves, *Multinational Enterprise and Economic Analysis*, Cambridge, Cambridge University Press, 1982; N. Hood, S. Young, *The Economics of Multinational Enterprise*, London, Longman, 1979.
4 L. Spalinski, 'Polonijne Forum Gospodarcze', *Zycie Warszawy*, Warsaw, 1990, 22 October, p. 1.
5 M. Rojec, *Some Results of Existing Joint Ventures in Yugoslavia*, Ljubljana, mimeo, CICD, 1990, p. 2.
6 M. Rojec, op.cit., p. 4.

3 EVOLUTION OF LEGAL REGULATIONS AND THEIR IMPACT ON FOREIGN INVESTMENT

1 *Investing in Yugoslavia*, Ljubljana, Center for International Cooperation and Development, 1990, p. 15.
2 Ibid., p. 12.
3 M. Svetlicic, M. Rojec, 'Technology Imports of Yugoslavia. The Case of Long-Term Cooperation with Foreign Partners', *Development and South–South Cooperation*, December 1988, No.7, p. 52.
4 *Foreign Investments Law*, Belgrade, 1988, Articles 9 and 17–21.
5 *Investing in Yugoslavia*, op. cit., p. 32.
6 G. Wujek (ed.), *How to Joint-Venture in Poland*, Warsaw, Polish Foundation, 1990, pp. 80, 81.
7 *Foreign Investor's Guide to Poland*, Warsaw, Foreign Investment Agency, 1990, pp. 14–15.
8 If the company engages in one of the preferred sectors of the economy, this tax holiday may be extended to six years.
9 *How to Joint-Venture in Poland*, op. cit., pp. 43–5.
10 *Foreign Investor's Guide to Poland*, op. cit., p. 20.
11 N. Denton, 'Hungary keeps tax breaks for foreign investors', *Financial Times*, 1990, October 20, p. 2.
12 M. Mejstrik, *The Transformation of Czechoslovakia to a Market Economy*, Prague, mimeo, October 1990, pp. 7–9.
13 *Economic, Business, Financial and Legal Aspects of East–West Joint Ventures*, Geneva, UNIDO, 1988.
14 *Foreign Investment Law*, mimeo, Bucharest, Parliament of Romania, April 1991, pp. 1–7.
15 L. Silber, 'Albania sets out to attract foreign investors', *Financial Times*, 1991, 2 January, p. 2.

4 REASONS FOR INVESTING IN EASTERN EUROPE

1 *Investing in Yugoslavia*, Ljubljana, CICD, 1990, p. 22.
2 J. Kwiatkowski, 'Zagraniczne inwestycje bezposrednie w krajach Europy Wschodniej', *Sprawy Miedzynarodowe*, 1990, No.1, p. 88.
3 J.M.C. Rollo et al., *The New Eastern Europe: Western Responses*, London, Pinter, 1990, pp. 107–8.
4 A.M. Rugman, 'Internationalization as a General Theory of Foreign Direct Investment: A reappraisal of the literature', *Weltwirtschaftliches Archiv*, 1980, No.116 (2), pp. 365–79.

128 *Notes*

5 *Financial Times*, 1990, 26 September, p. 12.
6 Forming ABB Dolmel and a second smaller company, Dolmel Drives, to make drives and traction motors.
7 *Zycie Warszawy*, 1990, 12 July, p. 2.
8 A. Rugman, D. Lecraw, L.D. Booth, *International Business*, New York, McGraw-Hill, 1985.
9 de A. Julius, *Global companies and public policy: the growing challenge of foreign direct investment*, London, Royal Institute of International Affairs/ Pinter, 1990.
10 *Les Sociétés transnationales dans le developpement mondial. Tendances et perspectives*, New York, UNCTC, United Nations, 1989, *passim*.
11 *Europe in 1994: Economic Outlook by Sectors*, Cambridge, 1990.

5 STRUCTURE OF FOREIGN INVESTMENT

1 *Foreign Direct Investment and Transnational Corporations in Services*, New York, UNCTC, United Nations, 1989, p. 8.
2 Foreign Investment Law, Articles 18 and 19.
3 *Financial Times*, 1990, 9 July, p. 14.
4 Ibid., p. 14.
5 *The Economist*, 1990, 30 June, p. 87.
6 K. Done, A. Fisher, 'VW and Skoda unveil DM 9.5bn strategy', *Financial Times*, 1990, 11 December, p. 19.
7 *Financial Times*, 1990, 17 July, p. 2.
8 *Foreign Direct Investments and Transnational Corporations in Services*, op. cit., p. 8.
9 *Fortune International*, 1990, 15 January, p. 30.
10 M. Sowa, 'Nie spelniony (na razie) sen o City nad Wisla', *Rynki Zagraniczne*, Warsaw, 1990, 17 May, p. 8.
11 Foreign Investment Law, Article 21.
12 E. Ben, 'Mozliwosci ekspansji zachodnioeuropejskich towarzystw ubezpieczeniowych w krajach RWPG', *Ekonomika i organizacja przedsieborstwa*, No.11, 1990, p. 13.
13 I. Grabowska, 'Ksiegowa prawde ci powie', *Polityka*, Warsaw, 1990, No.6, p. 19.
14 M. Tekielski, 'Ernst and Young TKD. Operating the World', *The Warsaw Voice*, 1990, 4 November, p. 13.
15 G. Fitzpatrick, 'Learn the Market', *The Warsaw Voice*, 1990, 9 December, p. 11.
16 'Franchising in Eastern Europe. McGoulash to go.', *The Economist*, 1991, 6 April, pp. 66 and 67.
17 H. Jezierski, 'Wojewoda w spolce', *Przeglad Tygodniowy*, Warsaw, 1990, No.25, p. 5.
18 B. Vukmir, 'Latest developments in the joint venture legislation in Eastern Europe', *The CTC Reporter*, 1989, No.28, p. 35.
19 L. Zmijewski, 'Telecommunications. Do Not Pass Go', *The Warsaw Voice*, 1990, 4 November, p. 5.
20 *Zycie Gospodarcze*, Warsaw, 1989, 26 March, p. 5.
21 M.T. Lynn, 'How Far Can You Go?', *The Warsaw Voice*, 1990, 4 November, p. 10.

6 GEOGRAPHY OF FOREIGN INVESTMENT

1 M. Rojec, *Recent Trends and Experiences in Foreign Investments in Yugoslavia*, Ljubljana, 1990, mimeo, p. 2.
2 Z. Takacs, J. Kristof, 'Vegvesvallalatok za iparban', *Figyelo*, 1990, 18 May, p. 18; *Boss*, 1991, No.39, p. 11.
3 M. Rojec, op. cit., p. 2.
4 Ibid., p. 9.
5 M. Svetlicic, M. Rojec, op. cit., p. 48.
6 *Zycie Warszawy*, Warsaw, 1991, 4 January, p. 6.
7 E. Sadowska-Cieslik, *Analysis of Licences Granted by Foreign Investment Companies*, Warsaw, Foreign Investment Agency, 1990, mimeo, Table 6.
8 *Transnational Corporations in World Development. Trends and Prospects*, New York, UNCTC, 1988, p. 301.
9 A. Blaho, 'Joint ventures in Hungary', *The CTC Reporter*, 1989, No.28, p. 38; *Boss*, 1991, No.39, 1991.
10 *Transnational Corporation in World Development. Trends and Prospects*, op. cit., p. 301.
11 Act XXIV (1988) on Foreign Investment in Hungary, paras 37–43.
12 'Zakon o slobodnim i carinskim zonam', *Official Gazette of SFRY*, 1990, No.3.
13 'Decree No.2242 on Free Trade Zones', *State Gazette*, No.55, 1987.
14 Ibid., Article 13.4.
15 'Decree No.56 on Economic Activity', *State Gazette*, No.72, 1989.

7 PORTFOLIO INVESTMENT

1 *Le Monde*, 1990, 24 July, p. 13; *Financial Times*, 1991, 5 June, p. 22.
2 J. Kwiatkowski, 'Papier w ruchu', *Przeglad Tygodniowy*, 1990, No.36, p. 9.
3 B. Rosen, 'For Investors Contemplating East Europe, Money is Time', *International Herald Tribune*, 1990, 29–30 December, p. 19.
4 L. Bokkros, *Privatization in Hungary*, Budapest, November 1990, mimeo, p. 5.
5 Ibid., p. 9.
6 Ibid., p. 10.
7 'Law on Social Capital', *Official Gazette of SFRY*, 1990, No.46, Articles 1 and 4.
8 *Law on Privatization of Companies*, Ljubljana, 1990, mimeo, Article 34.
9 Simon London, 'Yugoslav SE plans electronic settlement', *Financial Times*, 1990, 1 February, p. 20.
10 *Act on Privatization of State-owned Enterprises*, Warsaw, Ministry of Ownership Changes, 1990, mimeo.

Index

99–100; automobile industry, 73–4; broadcasting media, 87; ethnic tensions, 120; expatriate investment, 52–3; free trade areas, 106–7; French investment in, 29, 40, 73–4, 78, 96; German investment in, 81, 93–4; Italian investment in, 73; joint ventures, 40, 41, 87, 93, 99; labour productivity, 28; labour relations laws, 42; legal regulations, 39–42; 106; mineral resources, extraction of, 68; political change, 8; portfolio investment, 114–15; price structure, 13, 14; private sector, 10; privatization, 114; tax system, 41–2; technology transfer, 29; telecommunications, 85; UK investment in, 80, 95; unofficial economy, 11; US investment in, 97

Zamech, 32, 61
Zavodi Crvena Zastava (ZCZ), 73